The Lure of Far-Away Places

THE LURE OF
FAR-AWAY PLACES

*Maritime Tales of Adventures
Afloat and Ashore*

Norman Freeman

The Liffey Press

Published by
The Liffey Press Ltd
Raheny Shopping Centre, Second Floor
Raheny, Dublin 5, Ireland
www.theliffeypress.com

A catalogue record of this book is
available from the British Library.

ISBN 978-1-908308-75-7

Cover drawing by Alan Clarke

Printed in Spain by GraphyCems

CONTENTS

Contents

vii

Contents

FOREWORD

Most of the true tales in this book were first heard on RTE Radio 1's maritime programme, *Seascapes*, where they attracted an appreciative audience.

They are drawn from a time when Norman Freeman journeyed on vessels with highly qualified mariners drawn from around the seven seas as they enjoyed their time in the ports they visited, disembarking their guests or unloading their varied cargoes.

Relating the tale of Albert the Albatross, or the warthog bound for an expectant zoo, or the larger-than-life characters who undertook a life at sea, Norman recounts their many adventures in his own unique and inimitable style.

In the great maritime tradition of this island facing the brunt of the Atlantic weather systems, the name of Marconi is a hallowed one. Over several generations marine Radio Officers or R/Os were lauded and cherished for their lifestyles and tales of adventure on the high seas and ashore, wherever in the world their ships had sailed carrying passengers or cargo. Norman was one of these.

Norman was also one of the contributors to the publication *Sailing By,* which celebrated 25 years of *Seascapes* and which was launched recently at the National Maritime Museum of Ireland in Dun Laoghaire.

Marcus Connaughton
Writer and broadcaster
Presenter and producer of *Seascapes* –
The maritime programme on RTÉ Radio 1

1

THE IRISH BARBER AND
THE ENGLISH DUCHESS

The barber's chair put to unusual use

There was a barber near Baggot Street in Dublin who entertained customers with stories of his brief seafaring career. He's long since gone, his little shop knocked down, but his adventures remain in my mind.

I don't know how exaggerated this particular episode might be but both seafarers and barbers have to be allowed a certain leeway to embellish a yarn.

As a young man Mossie, a small, wiry fellow went to sea as a barber on a big British cruise liner, sailing to the Caribbean. He joined the ship in Southhampton. He was called a Gentleman's Hairdresser. The centrepiece of his saloon was a well-padded barber's chair; it could swivel about, be tilted this way and that, all for the comfort of the eminent passengers.

This was an exclusive class vessel long before cruise ships became popular with the masses. Mossie found that snobbery was rife. Passengers, mostly English, were exceedingly conscious of their class, their breeding and lineage.

As he was settling into his comfortable cabin he was summoned before the Passenger Administration Manager. This fellow, bloated with a sense of his own importance, stressed how respectful Mossie must be of the esteemed passengers who might want to get their hair cut. "You must treat them with the utmost courtesy. You must never become over-familiar with them, as some barbers might do."

Mossie, who came from a Cork republican background, just nodded but said nothing.

The most prominent of the distinguished passengers was a duchess. Mossie heard she was a close relative of the British royal family. He heard also that this beautiful woman was noted for her promiscuity and that she had recently been divorced by her second husband on the grounds of infidelity.

According to Mossie, about four days into the voyage she created the most appalling fuss in the women's beauty salon. She raged that her hair had not been properly cut and set. When she declared that she wanted her lower legs shaved none of the women staff would undertake this delicate task. They were afraid of her and her demanding manner.

Apparently she was striding along the deck in a state of rage when she noticed the Gentleman's Hairdressing Saloon and burst in. Mossie was there alone and greeted her with a "Howareyeh?". When she asked if he could shave her lower legs he said, "No bother. But it will have to be after hours."

That night after ten she knocked at the door of the closed saloon. When Mossie ushered her in, he became aware that she was well-oiled and in great good humour.

As she sat in the barber's chair taking off her tights she asked, "Is this your first time shaving a woman's legs?" He replied, "Oh it is. And what a beautiful pair to begin with."

She asked him where he was from. When he told her she exclaimed, "Oh I used to have cousins in Cork. Unfortunately the marquess was burned out of his mansion in 1921 by some chaps in the IRA."

"My father was probably one of them," was his response. To which she said as she settled herself into the chair, "We'll let bygones be bygones."

As his story goes, he knelt before her and shaved her lower legs with great care. When the job was done and he was rubbing in some after-shave lotion the duchess became amorous. She leaned forward, caught him by the hair of his head and pulled him towards her. She discarded some underwear and wrapped her newly-shaven legs round his waist. He was delighted with this turn of events. The barber's chair was being put to a use not envisaged by its designer.

For the following three nights she came there every night at ten.

"To tell you the God's honest truth I was put to the pin of my collar trying to keep up with her," said Mossie in recollection.

This dilemma, such as it was, was solved the next night. Apparently the Passenger Administration Manager was strolling about the deck when he noticed some movement through the window of the semi-darkened barber's saloon. He peered in. He was utterly shocked by the love-scene he witnessed.

Next morning he summoned Mossie to his office, told him he was to be replaced when the ship reached Kingstown in Jamaica. On condition that he keep quiet about this disgraceful escapade he would get his full wages as if he had completed the voyage and a passage back to the UK on a passenger ship.

The Manager was anxious that the other passengers on that class-ridden liner learned nothing of the episode. Were they to hear of it they would be absolutely appalled at the very notion of a relative of the royal family having a somewhat undignified liaison with the ship's Irish barber.

Only after he pocketed his money and his passenger ticket did Mossie say, "Listen, the tilting mechanism of the barber's chair needs to be repaired."

2

ART EXHIBITIONS WERE HIS HUNTING GROUNDS

Those bonded by art can be bonded by desire

The Third Engineer's romantic activities in New Orleans were a source of speculation, if not wonderment. Anyone around early in the morning would see a long limousine draw up on the dockside beside our shabby cargo ship. The Third would alight, blow a kiss to the elegant-looking woman at the wheel, and then make his way up the clattering gangway.

On another occasion a limousine was driven by a chauffeur wearing a peaked cap, who jumped out to open the door for our Third who emerged like some dignitary at a conference and headed over to our battered ship.

"How does he do it? How does he meet these high class women?"

This question was asked by our roistering, boisterous fellows who sought women in the noisy strip joints and smoke-filled night clubs and dockside dives. They found them but also found that money had to change hands for any sexual favours granted.

Some fellows got into rows over women in these disreputable places and staggered back to the ship in the small hours, nursing black eyes and skinned knuckles.

Others woke up in some seedy room to find that the woman had disappeared along with their wallet.

There were the usual doubtful stories from men who claimed to have become very close to the women they consorted with. "She's game ball. She's taken to me in a big way. I'm getting it free now."

The Third Engineer was different. He left the ship neatly dressed in blazer and well-pressed slacks, always wearing a silk cravat round his neck. He was not a handsome fellow by any means; he wore large bottle-lensed glasses, his hair was unruly and he had large tombstone teeth. But his manner was amiable and gentle.

One afternoon I went down to his cabin just to say hello to him. I found him with a red pencil in hand poring over announcements for artistic events in the leading city newspaper, *The Times Picayune*.

"I like to keep an eye on art exhibitions."

"Have you an interest in that sort of thing?"

"Not really."

The Third knew I was a quiet type who wouldn't go round blabbing.

He had found that art exhibitions were places where a painting or sculpture sometimes created a kind of bond between those looking at it. There were always some likely females to be chatted up. If they responded in a friendly way a fleeting romance might develop.

He had been lucky in New Orleans. There was an exhibition of modern art in a gallery. He said that late afternoon or early evening was the time when there was an influx of viewers. The first thing he did was to make sure the art gallery had a restaurant or coffee shop or bar.

Then he bought a catalogue of the exhibits, studied it at his leisure and began to stroll around the gallery or the rooms, keeping an eye out for any likely woman. There were always conferences going on in New Orleans and sometimes in the evenings delegates drifted into the art centre.

He would never try to get into conversation with a women standing in front of a nude picture or a piece of sculpture that resembled a penis. That would be too obvious.

He told me that on the first evening he saw a very good looking woman somewhere in her thirties making her way slowly along the exhibits. He went nimbly ahead of her and was standing with a frown of puzzlement on his face at a picture full of red, blue and green splashes.

This woman joined him and he turned to her and said, "It's supposed to be sunset over the Gulf of Mexico but I can't make it out."

She had responded warmly, "Neither can I."

They got talking about the picture. She was intrigued by his accent and asked him where he was from. They chatted and then he asked her if she'd like a cup of coffee.

He always kept to his rule never to suggest a drink. That might give the impression that he was too eager.

She was from New York, was staying for three days. She was taken by his manner.

I think there was something about him that made him attractive to women despite his less-than-handsome face. He was quiet and amiable. He listened carefully and sympathetically to what they had to say about themselves.

He spent three nights with her in her bedroom in a high-class hotel and she drove him back to the docks in her hired limousine.

Two days later he went to the same exhibition. He was lucky. He got chatting to a vivacious woman of early middle age before a painting of a predatory crocodile in a bayou. She responded eagerly to his invitation for a cup of coffee.

She proved to be a very wealthy woman who went about in a chauffer-driven car. She invited him to stay with her in a luxurious apartment. Maybe some of his attraction was that he came from a different world, a man who worked down in the thumping engine-room of a ship heaving and plunging it's way across rough seas.

Telling me of his romantic adventures he said: "In a funny way it's opened new worlds for me. I've begun to take an interest in art of all kinds, become curious about it."

He said that when he got back to Newcastle upon Tyne he intended to spend a lot of time going round the art galleries there.

"You never know, I might take up painting or sculpture myself. Or become an art dealer," he said, with a tombstone-toothed grin.

.

3

A LESSON IN DIGNITY

Goan servant showed how

When I awoke, after my first night's sleep in my cabin, I was slightly alarmed to find a thin, elderly, brown-skinned man standing there, dressed in a white cotton uniform.

"Good morning, Sahib. Here is your lime juice," he said, putting the glass on my desk. Then he tidied up the clothes I had thrown off the previous night, perspiring in the heavy tropical heat. I was very uneasy about anyone attending on me. I wasn't used to it. But I was afraid to ask him who he was because I was in a state of culture shock. I'd only arrived in Bombay, now called Mumbai, the previous day to join this ship as a Trainee Radio Officer. I'd never been far from our home in Omeath on the shores of Carlingford Lough. I was now overwhelmed by the stifling temperatures, the thousands of people thronging the streets dressed in white cotton, the pavements streaked with red betel nut juice, the smells of spices and burning wood, the endless honking of taxi and rickshaw horns.

And I'd never slept aboard a ship before. Everything was new to me – the wooden decks, the canvas awnings to provide shelter from the relentless sun, the shouts in strange languages from the bustling docks below.

Later there was a rap on the gauze door and a young fellow, dressed immaculately in white uniform shirt, shorts, shoes and cap put his head in. He spoke with a languid upper-crust English accent. His name was Rupert and he was a Cadet Deck Officer.

When I asked him about the elderly man in my cabin he said, "Oh that's Joaquim. He's your 'boy'. He serves myself and the Third Officer as well."

Joaquim came from Goa, then still a small Portuguese colony on the west coast of India. There was a tradition of men from there acting as stewards and servants on British ships.

I was to hear British officers looking for attention in the saloon or in the bar or out on deck calling out "Boy". They may have felt superior but Joaquim spoke Konkani and Marathi, and could get by in Portuguese, English and Hindi. I was never going to call this elderly man "boy".

However Joaquim insisted on calling me "sahib". I was uneasy about that. It was an Arabic-based word for "Mister" or even "Master" and had become a term of subordination under the British Raj.

He knew I was a raw youth, a total beginner. In a kind and unobtrusive way he gave me some guidance. Several tailors sat cross-legged outside the door of my cabin, competing to supply me with white uniforms. I went along with the one Joaquim recommended.

When we set off for Mombasa the monsoon was blowing hard. The decks rose and fell as our ship ploughed into the big waves. I became wretchedly seasick. For two days I couldn't face food in the saloon. But Joaquim brought tea and biscuits to my cabin and some egg sandwiches to the radio room before I began my night watch.

He told me that he had been at sea for forty years and that he had many grandchildren.

Rupert was in the habit of ordering Joaquim about in a loud, authorative voice. There was an unfortunate incident one day when Rupert was sitting in my cabin. Joaquim came in with the afternoon glass of lime juice but tripped and splashed some of it over my desk.

"Silly boy, silly boy," admonished Rupert.

To this day I regret that I hadn't the courage to confront him and say, "Don't talk to Joaquim like that."

However, Joaquim responded with admirable composure: "Not to worry, Sahib, not to worry, Sahib" he said in a soothing voice, as if he was calming a juvenile. With a cloth he slowly wiped up the spilled lime juice. He moved with an impressive sense of dignity.

Since then I sometimes wished that I had the same deep self-esteem that served Joaquim so well. It enabled him to retain his dignity and serenity despite his role as a steward and being called a "boy".

4

DRAMATIST OBSESSED
BY SEA LIFE

The words were awakward
but they rang true

It was said of Eugene O'Neill, accepted as America's great-est playwright, that he was obsessed and possessed by the sea. Sometimes, during his dark troubled moods, he would remark that he would rather be a seagull.

Son of an Irish actor from Kilkenny, he spent many summers in the family holiday home in the old port of New London, Connecticut. As a boy and adolescent he wandered about the wharves, endlessly watching ships being loaded and unloaded, fascinated by the talk of the seafarers and the dockers. He began to take an intense interest in the kind of lives they led.

After he was kicked out of Princeton University, he knocked about the waterfronts of the eastern seaboard of the United States, putting up in squalid lodgings, living a hand-to-mouth existence, coming into close contact with all the human flotsam and jetsam of port life.

In 1910 he shipped out as a seaman on cargo ships. He endured all the hardships of seafaring in those years. He absorbed the atmosphere of shipboard life, observing the effects of a hard existence on his fellow humans. Like many seafarers he got into the habit of heavy drinking.

His first play, *Bound East for Cardiff*, was about the unfulfilled longings of a dying sailor who had wanted to quit the sea and go to live inland, close to the earth. It was produced in a theatre that had been a fish warehouse on a wharf in Provincetown, Massachusetts. During that foggy opening night, the tide was full in and the small audience could get the smell of the sea, hear it washing under the timber foundations. O'Neill himself took on the small role of the Second Mate.

His dominating interest in seafarers and those who peopled the world of the waterfront – sailors, drifters, prostitutes, dockers – provided material for fifteen of his first twenty-five plays.

O'Neill had a very dismal view of life. He was subject to dark, depressive moods that were reflected in the pessimism that permeates his work. He went on binges.

Yet he wrote enthralling plays about real people and real life. For the first time in the American theatre the ordinary speech of human beings struggling to maintain their hopes was heard on stage. His characters tried to express their longings, their disappointments, their joy and sadness in words that were awkward but that rang true.

O'Neill's realism led to his being regarded as the father of all serious American drama. His disturbing but intriguing plays won the Pulitzer Prize on four occasions. And in 1936 he was awarded the Nobel Prize for literature, the only American playwright to be so honoured.

One of his most celebrated plays, *Long Day's Journey into Night*, is regularly seen in this country, produced by professional or amateur groups. Based on his own troubled family background, it is set in a house near the sea. During the course of the play the repeated moan of a foghorn is heard in the distance, intended to underline the loneliness and sadness that envelopes the characters.

Because of the constant moving of his theatrical family Eugene O'Neill was born in a hotel in New York in 1888. And, his own restless character resulted in his dying in a hotel in Boston in 1953. His last words were: "I knew it. I knew it. Born in a hotel room and God damn it, died in a hotel room."

Today, visitors to the waterfront of New London can see a statue of O'Neill as a schoolboy, looking thoughtfully at the dockside scene, with jotter and pencil to hand as if ready to jot down some of the ideas that he later turned into plays that still captivate audiences today.

5

A SPLENDID CAREER
AWAITS YOU

*"From now on I'm going
to study like a hoor."*

I suppose you could call this man a recruiting officer. He was tall, dressed in a well-cut, well-pressed tweed suit. When he entered our lecture theatre in the College of Science and Technology in Kevin Street, in Dublin, he looked at us in a masterful way.

We sat there on the worn, wooden tiers, looking respectfully at this impressive man with his bronzed face and wavy white hair. We were aged between seventeen and twenty-two, pale-faced, pimpled and mostly penniless.

We were studying for the Radio Officer's certificate, trying to master the intricacies of marine transmitters, receivers and radar and, equally important, the dots and dashes of the Morse Code. If we passed the exam it would mean going to sea as a radio officer.

At that time, in the 1950s, there was a boom in shipping. There was a shortage of radio officers and the Marconi Company was actively seeking men to join its ranks. That's why this distinguished personage from the head office in

Britain paid us a visit. His English accent added to his air of authority.

"Now chaps, as someone who spent twenty-five years at sea, I can tell you there's no better life." He looked out the window where a grey pall of rain was falling on the wet slates of the rooftops. "If you pass the exam and join the Marconi Company you'll find yourself in places where the sun is shining out of a blue sky, white beaches and palm trees – Rio de Janeiro, Sydney, Colombo."

The travel in our lives amounted to getting into the college on creaking bicycles or walking, often with collars turned up against cold and rain.

"In those places it's so warm people don't need to wear many clothes." His eyes twinkled roguishly, "And that includes many of the lovely young women you're bound to meet there."

The only women we noticed in the course of our day in college was the statuesque young woman from the admin office and the girl with the big round eyes and white coat who served behind the counter in the sweet shop nearby.

"Do many of you chaps smoke?" he asked.

Some of us nodded. Making cigarettes last a long time had become an art with us – lighting up, taking a few pulls and then extinguishing the fag between thumb and forefinger. The pockets of our shabby jackets reeked of stale cigarette butts.

He told us the good news. "At sea, tobacco is duty free. A tin of fifty cigarettes is only two shillings," He held up his right hand to display tobacco-browned fingers.

He continued enthusiastically. "And, of course, drink is duty free as well. A bottle of gin is only four shillings and sixpence. A bottle of whisky is only seven and six. Same with rum, vodka, brandy, beer."

A bottle of lemonade down in the sweet shop was about the extent of our drinking.

"And don't forget you'll be able to save when you're at sea. When you get to port you'll be walking down the street with money in your pocket, eyeing up the girls."

He had a wide pliant mouth and when he smiled he showed large white teeth.

"Oh Australia is a great place to meet women. I've a few addresses I might give you. But first of all," he held up his hand dramatically," first of all you have to pass your exam and join the Marconi Company."

With those words he bowed to the class and departed, like an eminent actor leaving the stage after a virtuoso performance. For a few seconds we sat there speechless.

Then a fellow from Dublin, who had been an indifferent student, stood up. He spoke earnestly, "Oh Jaysus, from now on I'm going to study like a hoor."

6

SHANGHAID TO MEET AN "EMERGENCY" IN INDIA

"Your boss is rather partial to gin."

The verb "to Shanghai" arose from a practice of tricking seafarers into signing on for what the shipping clerk described as a short voyage. However, when the ship got to a port like Shanghai the sailor found, to his dismay, that the vessel was now going to ply between there and other ports in China, Japan, the Philippines and Malaysia. He could be away for a good two years.

In the 1950s and 1960s, when shipping was booming, the Marconi Company supplied radio officers to shipping companies whose vessels stayed East of Suez. The British India company was one of these. Its offices were in Calcutta and Bombay and its ships ploughed back and forth to ports on the shores of the Indian Ocean, the Persian Gulf and the China Sea.

It was not always easy for the Marconi Company to find men willing to go out to India and not come home again for 18 months or longer, spending the time in stifling hot climates. So a certain amount of pretence and persuasion was necessary to get men to sign up.

It happened to me. I stood uneasily at the counter of the Marconi office in London, a raw youth who had just scraped past the examination for a marine Radio Officer's certificate. The appointments clerk, a small , wizened man, looked at my anxious face and then scanned a list of ships on a clipboard. I could be appointed to any of them to serve my apprenticeship as a junior.

He coughed in an authoritative way. "We have an emergency. Passenger ship in Bombay can't sail without a second radio officer."

An emergency! Immediately I felt valued, even a bit self-important.

"We'll fly you out in four days time," he said. I'd never been on a plane and a flight from London to Bombay sounded very exciting even though I hardly knew where India was on the globe.

Only when I was signing the contract did a faint note of caution enter my mind. "Will I be away for very long?" I asked the man timidly.

"Ah, no more than six months or so," he responded airily. "And there's a special East of Suez bonus."

Some days later I was on an Air India flight. After a long journey through the night we arrived at Santa Cruz airport some time in the afternoon. People milled about everywhere. Their faces were various shades of brown. They wore white cotton clothing. They gesticulated expressively as they spoke in rounded, well-sprung sing-song syllables.

On the bus to the city I noticed areas of poverty-stricken shanties and tumble-down shacks. The architecture and the monuments became impressive as we neared the city centre. Yet I saw skinny bony cows wandering about the streets and doubted if this could be the terminus. Then the bus stopped and a man with a big moustache knocked at the window and gestured to me to get out.

This turned out to be John Mendes, the Assistant Purser on board the ship *Amra*, of the British India company. I was glad to be taken into his welcoming care because I was more than a bit bewildered with culture shock, the sounds, the claustrophobic heat, the smells, the thousands of people walking along the footpaths and streets, the endless cascade of taxis and rickshaws.

We drove down to the Ballard pier where the white-painted vessel was berthed. The *Amra* was a deck-passenger ship that never left the Indian Ocean, plying back and forth between India and the East African ports of Mombasa, Dar Es Salaam and Zanzibar.

My cabin was up on the boat deck. I had never been in a ship's cabin before. I slowly stowed away my clothes and meagre belongings. I tested the settee and patted the sheet on my bunk beside the bulkhead. Then I sat down at the escritoire to write a letter to my mother in Omeath, on the shores of Carlingford lough. With some pride I told her that I'd been flown out to India to meet an emergency but that I would be back home in six months or so.

Then the Third Mate, a genial English fellow, appeared. With a wide grin he told me that the Chief Radio Officer had been at loggerheads with the junior during the previous voyage. They had almost come to blows. The junior had to go. I was replacing him. That was the emergency.

"Your boss is rather partial to gin," he said, chuckling.

With all this in mind I stepped warily round to the starboard side to the Chief's cabin. When I peered in through the wire-mesh door I could see this pink figure sprawled on his back on the settee. He was fast asleep. He was clad in nothing but his underpants. His dentures were out and his mouth was no more than a black sunken hole. On the coffee table was an empty bottle of Gordon's Gin.

As it turned out, I got on quite well with him. He could be bad tempered when he had a hangover, which was often, but he had a lively Belfast sense of humour and could use colourful and obscene language with great style and wit.

The following evening I was invited to a get-together of radio officers who were attached to the Bombay office of the Marconi Company. It was held aboard one of the passenger ships of the Mogul line berthed nearby. When I entered the lounge someone shouted, "Oh, here's another poor fellow sent out into the arms of Mother India for a long, long spell."

When I replied, innocently, "I'm only here for about six months," there was a spontaneous burst of laughter.

Most of them had been out there 18 months and some of them for two years and more. It was a full three years before I saw the shores of Carlingford Lough again.

7

WHEN CATS WERE PART OF THE CREW

Cat that survived wartime sinkings

There's a long history of cats being carried on ships. The ancient Egyptians took cats on board their Nile sailing boats in order to catch birds in the bushes along the river banks.

Cats were carried on trading ships in the ancient world to keep rodents in check. This led to the spread of domesticated cats in those parts of the world accessible by ship. Phoenician vessels are thought to have brought the first cats to Western Europe about 900 BC.

Many myths about cats were held by the usually superstitious seafaring community. They were supposed to have some supernatural powers that could protect ships from dangerous weather. It was believed to be a lucky omen if a cat approached a sailor on deck.

As well as that they were considered to be intelligent and lucky animals. Some of the beliefs about them are realistic. Cats are able to sense slight changes in the weather because of their acutely tuned inner ears. Low atmospheric pressure, a usual indication of stormy weather, often makes cats nervous and restless.

In modern times the main role of shipboard cats was for pest control. They hunted the mice and rats that found their way on board ships, gnaw at ropes and woodwork, and pilfer food, especially cargoes of grain. These rodents could also be carriers of disease; so the marine cat was expected to be a keen hunter.

Apart from that, cats also provided a form of companionship for sailors.

One of the most publicised cats in modern times was called Blackie. He was the mascot on the British battleship *The Prince of Wales*. At the start of World War Two this vessel was one of the most modern and formidable warships afloat.

In August 1941 she carried the British Prime Minister, Winston Churchill, to Newfoundland to meet US President Franklin D. Roosevelt. When Churchill was disembarking, with the sailors standing to attention as a guard of honour, Blackie came forward along the deck towards him. Churchill stooped down and rubbed its head.

A photo was taken of this gentle act. The British propaganda machine sent it all round the world. It contrasted with photos of the harsh, manic face of the rival war lord, Adolf Hitler, with his fearsome-looking Alsatian. In honour of the event the cat was renamed Churchill. I don't know if it was on board a short time later when the battleship was attacked and sunk by Japanese warplanes off the east coast of Malaya.

Another famous cat went to sea on board the *Bismark*, Germany's most famous battleship in World War Two.

When the huge warship was sunk by the British in 1941, the cat was among 116 survivors out of a crew of 2,200.

He was found floating on a board and picked up by the British destroyer *Cossack*. The crew named him Oscar. A few months later the *Cossack* itself was sunk by a German torpedo, losing 159 of her crew. Again the cat survived.

Now called Unsinkable Sam, he became the ship's cat of the aircraft carrier *Ark Royal*. This warship was in turn torpedoed and sunk. Sam clung to a plank and was picked up by a motor launch. Someone with dry English humour described him as "angry but unharmed".

After that it was decided that he'd had enough war-time adventures. He was given a home in the offices of the Governor in Gibraltar. He was later sent to the UK and actually ended up living in a seaman's home in Belfast. He died there in 1955.

A pastel portrait of him, entitled "Oscar, the Bismark's cat", by artist Georgina Shaw-Baker hangs in the National Maritime Museum in Greenwich, outside London.

8

MASTERPIECE OF THE SEA BY "BOAT HAPPY" WRITER

Hemingway and his love for Pilar

The American writer and adventurer Ernest Hemingway had a long devotion to a fishing boat. It was a prize possession. In 1934, when he was at the height of his renown as an author, he bought a 38-foot vessel with powerful engines and a flying bridge. It was designed for big seas and big fishing. It was called *Pilar*.

From his home in Havana, Cuba, he went out to sea to fish the deep waters of the Caribbean. He was after giant blue-fin tuna, broadbill swordfish and blue marlin. Fighting such huge combative fish called for stamina and courage. For Hemingway, obsessed with displaying a macho personality, deep sea fishing became more a way of life than a sport.

He took great pride in teaching his three sons to grapple heroically with these massive fish. Using his considerable strength, he pulled these fish into the boat before they tired, thereby preventing sharks taking slices out of them.

On other occasions his inherent violence resulting from his disturbed personality came to the fore. When sharks attacked his catch he got out his Tommy gun and riddled them with bullets, turning the sea red.

Numerous guests, including friends, relatives and celebrities, joined him on these fishing trips. Sometimes they were out at sea for days. Copious amounts of alcohol were drunk, with Hemingway himself taking pride in the amount of drink he could hold.

A powerfully built man, his aggressive nature sometimes turned him into a bully and a bar-room brawler, challenging people to fist fights and boxing matches.

A recently published book, *Hemingway's Pilar*, by Paul Hendrickson, uses the writer's deep association with the boat to trace his life from 1934 to his death in 1961.

In it Hemingway is described as being incurably "boat happy." He was addicted to being on board as much as possible.

When he married for the third time, he and his new wife, the American journalist Martha Gellhorn, celebrated with parties on board the *Pilar* and in the harbour bars. But his boorishness and increasingly heavy drinking scuttled the marriage.

The critics that had lionised him for the books that had made him famous, *The Sun Also Rises* and *A Farewell to Arms*, wondered if all the alcohol and adventuring had ruined his writing career.

Yet in 1951 he write a book that came out of his daily experience on his boat, *The Old Man and the Sea*. In it an elderly Cuban fisherman, wrinkled and browned by years under the sun, goes far out to sea, seeking a good catch. Hemingway paints a memorable picture of a brave but gentle soul, alone in his small boat on the vast ocean, with white clouds reaching up to the heavens.

He eventually hooks a giant marlin and battles doggedly with it for hours until he finally manages to tie it to the side of his small craft, but he could not prevent the sharks from reducing the hard-won prize to a skeleton. Yet the old man's spirit is intact because he has struggled courageously.

This book won Hemingway the Nobel Prize and he again achieved world acclaim. However he was suffering from bouts of depression and paranoia, and his drinking got worse. He became unhinged. In 1961 he took a gun from his hunting armoury and killed himself.

His reputation declined over the years but there has been a revival of interest in his books. Meanwhile, the boat that saw him through three marriages, years of alcoholism as well as several books, is now on display in the Museo Ernest Hemingway at Finca Vigia, the writer's former home near Havana. It must be rare that a person's fishing boat is the centre-piece of a museum dedicated to their memory.

9

A HUGE GASH ALONG THE UNDERSIDE OF THE SHIP

"Now we really know what going on the rocks is like."

Going on the rocks can happen in the most unexpected way. In August 1963 our cargo ship, the *Wairangi* of the Shaw Saville line, reached the outskirts of Stockholm. It was at the end of a long voyage from South America to Europe. We felt that we had reached journey's end.

The pilot came on board about midnight. After I shut the radio room I went up on the bridge to watch him taking our ship through the tortuous black waterway, with its many navigation beacons blinking in the darkness.

He kept calling out to the man at the wheel, "two degrees port", "two degrees starboard", "one degree port". His voice had a monotonous, even mesmerising effect.

I was sound asleep in my bunk at about 2.00 am when awoken by a great shaking movement. The ship groaned and shuddered. The engines seemed to go astern and then stopped. Then the alarm bells echoed along all the passageways.

I raced up to the radio room. The Second Mate dashed in to tell me we had gone on an outcrop of rocks called Kloveholmen. He gave me the ship's position. "There's a danger she may break her back," he called as he ran out the door.

The pilot was already talking to the port authorities in Stockholm on VHF, but I had to alert the Swedish marine radio stations on medium wave.

While I was hammering away on the Morse key I noticed the calendar on the bulkhead moving sideways. Then a pencil rolled across the desk that was beginning to slope. Next thing I heard shouts of command and then came the rattling sound of the davits as the lifeboats were being lowered. When you've duties to perform, when you're busy, you haven't time to feel afraid.

Afterwards, I heard what had happened. The Swedish pilot had kept calling out the changes to the able seaman on the wheel, so many degrees to starboard, so many degrees to port, back and forward, on and on and on. It seems the wheelsman lost concentration just at the end of his watch. He went to starboared instead of to port. The pilot shouted out but it was too late. We crunched onto the rocks.

I heard later that as the wheelsman left the bridge he said, "Sorry about that, Captain."

The Captain retorted, "So you bloody well ought to be."

Before dawn broke two Swedish tugboats and two large rescue vessels had arrived and were standing by. It was reckoned that there was no danger of our ship breaking her back, and in mid-morning the lifeboats and those in them were lifted up.

Despite several efforts by the Swedish tugs to pull us free, with the ship's engines going full astern, we remained pinioned on those rocks.

After five or six days stuck there, our salvation appeared in the form of an enormous tugboat from the world's most famous salvage operation, Smits of Rotterdam. It was, most appropriately, called *Goliath*.

Everyone on board was on standby as the hardy Dutchmen put big steel cables around us. At a given word our engines were put full astern. The thumping thunder of *Goliath's* engines could be heard for miles around. The water churned white. Then suddenly we felt our ship slide back into the water. To a collective sigh of relief we were afloat once again.

Accompanied by *Goliath* and two Swedish tugs we made our way slowly up to Stockholm. There our wounded ship was put into dry dock.

When the water drained out we went down to view the damage. It was if a massive can opener had ripped an enormous gash along the underside of our ship. It was no surprise to hear that the vessel was considered a write-off.

Our Captain, Derek Aberdeen, a very fine man, said, "Well, from now on, the phrase 'going on the rocks' will mean something to us."

10

FAMOUS DARTBOARD FOUND A "HOME" IN WEST AFRICA

Once at the centre of extraordinary competitions

A dilapidated dartboard hung on the panelled bulkhead in the recreation room of our grubby cargo ship.

While we were docked in Liverpool games got under way when fellows came back from the pubs. Players squinted at the board from glazed eyes or had to make efforts to keep steady on their feet. Our tubby Captain was one of the best performers because he could hold his drink.

Then in mid-winter we set off into the North Atlantic, bound for New York. Our small ship got a bad buffeting from storms in that dark turbulent sea. After eight or nine days the sea got less rough. Just the same the deck still rose and fell and yawed. Anyone might think it was impossible to play darts under such conditions.

But on Chrismas Eve there was an amazing session that must be unique in the history of the game. The recreation room was packed. It was blue with tobacco smoke. A strong smell of whisky wafted about. Beer cans were everywhere.

Our stout bandy-legged Captain was throwing, feet apart to counter the movement of the ship, his beer belly seeming to act as a stabiliser. He blew out his cheeks theatrically, eyeing the target from beneath bushy eyebrows. Grinning at the challenge, he waited until the dartboard rose or fell to come level with his eyes. Then at the precise split second, with a deft flick of his thick hairy wrist, he flung each dart with a flourish. He was content with a modest score.

An exceptional display of skill against the odds was provided by the Third Engineer, a fellow with tousled hair and bottle-lensed glasses. He showed extraordinary mastery of the heaving and rolling deck. He didn't always wait for the board to come to eye-level. He flung the darts with uncanny accuracy. Several times he hit the treble twenty. Undoubtedly, he was helped to win by the fact that he was completely sober whereas most of the other contestants were alcoholically handicapped.

These dart games on the high seas at Christmas made all subsequent competitions played when the ship was in port look very ordinary. There wasn't the same challenge, the same excitement.

When we eventually returned to the UK our fellows told friends, families and other seafarers and pub audiences about the extraordinary games. When the Third Engineer's family came on board they crowded into the recreation room to see the dartboard. A photograph was taken of him standing beside it.

The Third Mate's father, a hearty, red-faced man, declared that the famous dartboard be donated to the National Maritime Museum in Greenwich, London as an exhibit.

That didn't happen. It was there for our next voyage to several ports in West Africa and Nigeria. Dart games were played whenever our ship was a few days in port.

When we got to Port Harcourt in eastern Nigeria two girls came on board, They were tall and dark-skinned with big round eyes. They spoke English with soft, slow accents. Of course they were offering love for sale but they had an exotic attraction. The Third Mate was taken by one of them and she spent the night in his cabin.

Our Purser, an amiable fellow who was pleasantly drunk a good deal of the time, had the other girl in his cabin for the night. However, in the morning it turned out that he hadn't enough money to pay the agreed amount. The girl got very annoyed. The Purser took her to the kitchen offering her bags of sugar and salt to make up the shortfall but she refused.

Still arguing, they went into the recreation room. She spotted our dartboard,

"I take this," she said.

"But that's the ship's dartboard. You can't have that."

"I take this," she repeated, removing it from the bulkhead.

"It's not worth a rex. It's falling apart."

For whatever reason, the girl felt that it was an object of some value and insisted on claiming it as part payment. The Purser didn't feel like pulling it out of her hands. It was carried down the gangway under the girl's arm.

Word quickly got round the ship about the fate of the dartboard. There was some anger. Regular players berated the Purser. The Captain was very annoyed and threatened to deduct a good sum of money from his wages. We were sailing next day and there was no chance to replace it.

The Third Mate said, "We should make an entry in the ship's log, 'Ship's dartboard bartered for carnal services.' When I tell my father he'll chuckle. Instead of it on exhibit in the Maritime Museum alongside the uniform coat of Admiral Lord Nelson and the sextant of Captain Cook, it's hanging on the wall of the waiting room of some whore-house in Africa."

11

ROMEO OF THE PERSIAN GULF

"I think she's fallen for me in a big way."

Our Second Officer, a charming English fellow, sought romance at every opportunity. Before passengers boarded he would go down to the purser's office and scrutinise the passenger list. Unaccompanied women travelling First Class aroused his interest.

Our ship, the *Sirdhana*, was a deck-passenger ship on the route from Bombay to Basra, there and back and many ports in between. We carried many from the Indian subcontinent who worked in places like Muscat, Dubai, Sharjah, Abu Dhabi, Kuwait as well as Iran and Iraq.

We also carried a small number of First Class passengers, mostly British, who lived or worked in the region.

Nobody better than our ship-board Romeo knew that a voyage in hot climates often led to Europeans throwing over the traces. There was a sense of freedom from the constraints of shore-side living. Men drank too much in the bar after dinner. Some women were not averse to a brief shipboard romance with a handsome ship's officer.

When the passengers came on board the Second Officer would hang round the reception area. He looked impressive in his white tropical uniform and his cap tilted at

35

a jaunty angle. He had developed an instinct that helped him to sense which women were most likely to respond to his genial approaches.

He had an amiable manner and he didn't find it difficult to strike up a flirtatious rapport with some likely woman. There were always one or two atttactive women and a few well-seasoned types who had played the love game before.

He was a very likeable fellow, popular on our ship, but he was inclinded to be boastful. He was always anxious to stress that these shipboard liaisons were not just releases of passionate energies. He'd often say, "Oh she's fallen for me in a big way."

One boarding day in Bombay, a very striking English woman was among the passengers. She had flaming red hair and a flamboyant manner. We all watched her as she went about the deck and into the saloon at meal times. Apparently she lived in Bahrain and had been visiting friends in India.

At first opportunity the Second Officer got chatting to her. Although listed as "Mrs" on the passenger list he noticed that she was not wearing a wedding ring. She responded very well to his jovial advances.

After several get-togethers for lime juice on the promenade deck in the morning, or a drink in the bar, she asked him, "Will I see you in the bar after dinner?"

He told her that he went on watch on the bridge at midnight and had to get sleep before that.

"What time do you come off watch?"

"Four a.m."

"Give a gentle knock on my cabin door. I'll have a beer or a gin and tonic waiting for you."

Not long after 4.00 a.m, passing by the radio room where I was on duty, he winked knowingly in my direction. A few hours later he returned, grinning and said, "Oh, she's fallen for me in a big way."

Their love affair continued as we made our way up the Persian Gulf. Our Romeo was beginning to talk as if it was becoming a serious affair. "She's a very fine woman. I could see us making a good couple."

Then, on the night before we reached Bahrain, she said to him, "I have something to tell you." He imagined he was going to hear a passionate declaration of undying love. Instead she told him that she was married to an Englishman working there.

"Oh, he is a decent sort of chap but rather dull. He sits smoking his pipe and reading when he comes home from work." Then she gave the Second Officer a peck on the cheek and said, "Thanks for your attention."

In Bahrain the Second Officer stood on the lifeboat deck and peeped down to the dockside. He watched as a tall, elderly man in white cotton gave the English woman a brief embrace and led her away.

Romeo was a bit deflated. "I thought she'd fallen for me," he said.

The Chief Officer, a sharp-witted Londoner, said: "He thinks he's God's gift to women. All some of them want from him is a certain part of his anatomy."

12

THE PIER AND THE PLATFORM

Taking the emigrant boat

In the 1950s the Carlisle pier in Dun Laoghaire was a place of sad, strained bustle. Every day passenger ships belonging to British Rail steamed into the harbour and then drew alongside. The gangways went rattling down. In the dismal concrete sheds hundreds of emigrants waited to board.

The *Hibernia* and the *Cambria* were two of the ships that for many were part of one of the most draining and nation-damaging periods of emigration since the aftermath of the Great Famine. They were notoriously uncomfortable and shoddy vessels. They rolled and yawed in any kind of a rough sea and passengers had to endure heaving decks. The sound of retching and the smell of vomit was often part of the short but trying voyage.

Over a ten-year period they carried thousands of emigrants across the Irish Sea to the port of Hollyhead in Wales. They often arrived there at night and the passengers poured off anxiously to find seats in the shabby trains that waited on the platforms under dim lights. The laden trains pulled out, rumbling into the night towards the big cities of Britain – Manchester, Liverpool, Birmingham, London.

Trains to the Carlisle pier left from a special platform at Pearse railway station in Dublin.

Today it's a tarmacadamed area beside the huge red-bricked wall, under the station's vast canopy of glass panes and iron struts.

This platform was once one of the busiest in the Irish railway system during the great exodus. Thousands of young Irish people had no option but to emigrate in search of a job and, perhaps, a better life. I was among them as a seafarer, travelling to Britain to join ships.

These eager, fresh-faced ones came off provincial trains and buses, wearing thick coats, hauling heavy suitcases, anxiously asking anyone in a railway uniform where the boat train platform could be found. They came from every part of the country; all the distinctive county and regional accents could be heard as they stood in line to buy their train tickets, dragging their cases forward as the queue shuffled onwards.

The men looked awkward in their plain suits. The girls wore little make-up; a ribbon or a small modest hat was all that adorned their hair. These were not seasoned travellers. Many had never been in Dublin before. They were unsure of what lay ahead. They hurried onto the platform and went on board.

They sat in the compartments with their cases on the racks or, for better safekeeping, on their knees. They exchanged questions. "What part are you from? Where are you heading for? Have you someone to meet you?"

The optimism of youth showed itself in jokes and laughter. They seemed light-hearted, as if looking forward to a new life in a land they really knew little about. The faces of these young men and women were suffused with hope.

But behind the smiles there was sadness. The recent good-byes to their loved ones at little railway stations, or by the side of the road when the bus appeared, were still in their minds. And, as the train began to move away, amidst the talk and banter was a strain of bitterness that their country could not offer them any kind of living. One of the most commonly used phrases of disillusionment was, "Sure, there's nothing for anyone in this country".

Many of that "generation of sad goodbyes" had no more than the minimum education. Menial and labouring jobs were all that they were qualified to do. Yet, on those trains and ships were some who would do well, but most would settle into dull jobs in the crowded cities of England.

Few would return to settle back in Ireland. However, they would come back on holidays to meet their families. And for funerals. They earned a reputation for hard and conscientious work. Many laboured in the building trades. Some did very well in other jobs. But not all. Loneliness and estrangement were challenges not everyone could handle; some turned to alcohol or turned away from life.

Most of these enforced emigrants sent money home. They helped their families to get by. They were decent people. They became know as "The Forgotten Irish".

On the East Pier in Dun Laoghaire there's a plaque to their memory. Perhaps another plaque should be affixed to the red-brick wall in Pearse station. The inscription might read:

> *"From this platform departed many young Irish men and women who had no alternative but to seek work abroad. They were faithful to their kith and kin. Their contributions helped the country through a difficult time."*

13

HATEFUL RIVALRY IN THE SOUTH PACIFIC

"How dare you say a thing like that."

The wooden promenade deck of our twelve-passenger cargo ship was the scene of contests of the most acrimonious rivalry between two of our passengers.

The deck was inlaid with two sets of concentric brass circles that were positioned about twelve yards apart. These marked the scoring ranges for the game of deck quoits, where small rope rings were pitched at the bulls-eye.

We had picked up our first five or six passengers in New York for our long journey to Australia. Among them was an Englishman who had been a senior civil servant based in London all his life. He spoke with a hoarse, weary accent.

He and his wife had flown to New York and spent a week there. They hadn't been very impressed with the people they met. These brash Yankees knew little about London or England, and had little desire to learn about it.

We later docked at Savannah, Georgia to pick up cargo and a few more passengers. Among them was an American couple, loud in their talk and laughter. The man, just retired, had apparently been a very successful businessman.

The captain said, "I'll put them at my table in the saloon. Maybe they'll act as some sort of counterweight to that boring English couple."

This turned out to be a bad seating arrangement. These two couples took an instant dislike to one another. Just as the English couple were overbearingly proud of being English, the American couple were boastful about the United States, its power and its virtues.

At first this rivalry in national fervour was expressed in off-hand remarks at meal times. Then the squabbles were transferred out to the bar after meals. Soon the exchanges became heated and bad-tempered.

As if to test the Englishman's mettle, the American challenged him to a game of deck quoits, at 20 dollars a game. The English fellow, determined to uphold the superiority of his blessed race, accepted. They and their wives went out on deck like gladiators under the hot tropical sun of the South Pacific.

The rivals stood intently on the marks and carefully pitched the rings, hoping to get them as near as possible to the bulls-eye. Their wives, sitting on opposite sides of the deck in deck-chairs, clapped their spouses on and remained sullenly silent when the rival player went into action.

Soon the games began to get rancorous. Arguments broke out about the exact position of the rope rings in relation to the circles and the bulls-eye. One afternoon, the American, in a loud combative voice, accused the Englishman of cheating by overstepping the mark when throwing his quoits.

"How dare you accuse me of cheating!" replied his rival.

"Play the goddam game right, for God's sake," the American shouted back.

The English fellow responded with some insulting remark. The American lost his temper and threw a rope ring at his opponent. It missed. But now the Captain intervened. "In the interests of international harmony, these games of quoits must come to an end," he said, commandingly.

The rival couples never spoke to one another again. They now sat at different tables in the saloon. They avoided one another in the bar and on deck. But ours was a small ship and it took great adroitness for them to avoid eye-contact or brushing against one another.

For us it was a form of entertainment to watch their rancour-driven behaviour. Eventually, when we got to Australia, they left the ship without a word of goodbye to one another.

Our Captain, watching them go down the gangway, said: "Us seafarers are not like that shower. We might not like one another but we have to work together to get the ship safely from point A to point B."

14

DARING DOCTOR WHO LIVED OFF THE SEA

"Nobody should ever starve in a lifeboat."

Over sixty years ago a small, round-faced Frenchman astonished the world. He set out alone to cross the Atlantic without food or water. Dr Alain Bombard wanted to prove that it was possible to survive by living off the sea.

A medical doctor and biologist who worked in a coastal hospital, he knew that thousands whose vessels sunk actually died, even after they had gained the safety of a lifeboat. They died of thirst and starvation.

Bombard was convinced that many of these deaths were avoidable. While rainwater was the obvious answer to thirst, he believed that drinking small amounts of sea water could sustain the body for up to five days without ill effect.

He also knew that a fish's body was made up of between 60 and 90 per cent water. Any fish caught by those in a lifeboat could provide both a thirst-quenching liquid and some nutrition.

Bombard studied the living organisms in sea water, knowing that some whales fed off the plankton that floated on the oceans. How to harvest this source of energy and nourishment occupied his mind. He then came up with the idea of a fine net trawling behind the boat that would collect enough plankton to add vitamin C to his diet.

News got round that this man intended to brave the Atlantic without anything to eat or drink in a rigid inflatable dinghy with a rudimentary sail and rudder. He was derided in France and called Dr Fool.

Aptly he called the small vessel *l'Heretique* to emphasise his determination to counter the widely felt pessimism about survival in a lifeboat. He left the Canary Islands in October 1952. The only back-up he had was a first-aid medical kit and survival rations sealed in the bottom of the craft in case of emergency. He took with him an ordinary fruit press to squeeze the nutritious liquid out of any fish he caught.

Unable to land any fish on the first six days, he survived on small amounts of sea water. Then, with a makeshift harpoon made of a knife bound to an oar, he caught a dorado – a large, dolphin-like fish. Not alone did it provide him with liquid and food but one of its bones was shaped like a fish-hook. Bombard used this at the end of a fishing line. He never went hungry after this. In addition, he swallowed some of the plankton sludge he dredged every day.

This courageous man endured some heavy seas and gales in his small craft. There were times it was nudged by sharks, swordfish and even a curious whale.

After eight weeks a British ship sighted him and gave him his position in the ocean. He was still 965 kilometres from land. After another two weeks at sea he eventually landed in Barbados on 23 December, having completed a journey of 4,400 kilometres.

He had lost about 25 kilogrammes, or four stone, and his body was covered in a rash. But he had survived.

His feat won him world-wide renown. It emphasised that it was possible to sustain life at sea if you knew how to set about it.

Bombar's story and his theories were not accepted everywhere; it was even suggested that he must have taken some fresh water with him. However, there was no denying his grit and determination in setting out alone on an immense journey across the Atlantic. His achievement underlined the fact that will and resolve, as well as knowing how to live off the ocean, could help those who found themselves in a lifeboat far from land.

15

WHAT DO YOU MEAN BY "SEA LEGS?"

Our captain had them for sure

The Third Mate and I were walking back to the ship along the wet pavements in the drizzling rain when he said: "There's the Old Man, up ahead. He has a walk like Popeye."

Our Captain walked along in a wide-legged gait, as if he expected the pavement to tilt this way or that. He was a low-slung, barrel-chested man with sturdy legs who had spent almost all his life at sea.

Undoubtedly he had what are called "sea legs". I watched him during our voyage in the stormy North Atlantic in winter and saw the ability he had to hold his balance on the rolling, yawing deck.

It was as if he had some inward sense of the height and frequency of the oncoming waves, even when he was in the chartroom or in the saloon at meal times.

He knew when to brace himself, to shift his weight from one foot to the other, to hold on to a rail, to put his hand against a bulkhead.

It was all second nature to him. But more than that he seemed to enjoy the deck heaving and falling. He had a cheerful grin on his round brown face. He often stood out on the wing of the bridge with a big beret pulled over his bald head, facing the gale and the spray with a jolly resolve.

Eventually we reached North America and then headed down to the Gulf of Mexico. It was warm and sunny with fairly placid seas as we headed for New Orleans.

"Ah, this isn't really a sea," he said in a sort of dismissive way, even though he knew that hurricanes roared through here in the summer season.

We were still 100 miles from the outlet of the Mississippi River when he said he could feel the sea bed under his feet despite it being a long distance below. He wasn't comfortable with it. Then the colour of the water changed to a light brown as we neared the mouth of the delta and our captain was uneasy as we entered relatively shallow waters. I wondered if he had gone aground some time in his past and had a lingering fear of it happening again.

He certainly felt ill at ease when the pilot came on board and guided us up the river to New Orleans. He felt the same many days later when another pilot came on board to take us down river.

When we got into the open sea he went to the wing of the bridge and inhaled gulps of fresh sea air. "That river and them old bayous and swamps. No place for a ship," he said.

However we were heading for Galveston in Texas and from there were to go up the canal to the port of Houston. He must have been one of the most reluctant mariners to take the pilot on board and to begin a fifty mile journey on a canal along a flat plain under a strong sun.

He joked and bantered with the gum-chewing pilot, but I felt he was putting on a show because he felt uneasy away from the open sea. His sea legs could gauge the depth of water beneath our keel and it made him unsettled.

After Houston we went back to New Orleans and then called to Mobile and Tampa. Then we headed south east to get round the tip of Florida and out into the North Atlantic ocean.

We weren't any more than a few days ploughing along that turbulent sea when the wind rose and howled through the rigging. The waves increased in size. More than that, it began to get cold.

The sea, however stormy, was deep beneath our captain's feet. He stood out on the wing of the bridge with his beret clamped on his head and with a look of contentment on his face. He was in his element.

16

THE POSITIVE POWER
OF SNAKE BITE

"Pity he wasn't bitten at the start of the voyage."

The cook on our down-at-heel cargo ship was a decent enough sort of fellow, but he drank a lot and as a result the food was often badly cooked.

We were served up with greasy stews. Meat was either underdone or almost burned. Vegetables were often reduced to a soggy pulp. At breakfast the fried eggs were reduced to small hard yolks with the whites singed brown round the edges; the rashers were often fried into hard wafers.

The Chief Engineer, who had developed an intense dislike of the man said, "It takes a cook of particular genius to spoil the simple English breakfast."

Even the Captain, who wolfed down anything put before him, once complained, "This bacon's hard as a whore's heart."

Our cook, a small, ferrety-faced man, was made bad tempered and combative by the words of criticism flung at him by members of the crew. Some of it was not deserved because he could only use whatever supplies were in the ship's storeroom and larder.

This was the fault of the Chief Steward, a good-natured man who was pleasantly pickled a good deal of the time. Both of them were blamed for the poor fare. It didn't help their status on board that they were regular drinking companions.

We picked up cargo in Antwerp and Hamburg and then set off for West African ports. The sea in the Bay of Biscay was turbulent. In the galley the cook, cursing and swearing, grappled clumsily with pots and pans and found it difficult to hold his feet.

The Chief Engineer said, "That's the advantage of a rough sea – it helps to hide the fact that the man is falling about the place drunk."

We called at the ports of Freetown, Conakry. Abidjan and Accra before going on to Port Harcourt in Nigeria. There, as a relief from the food on board, some fellows in our crew were tempted to go ashore and sample some of the local specialities. They returned to the ship blowing out their cheeks, racing to get a cold beer to lighten the effect of explosively hot chillies, peppers and spices.

"I don't know which is worse," they said.

Our last port of call before heading back to the UK was Sapele, a good distance up the Benin river. We were to load mahogany logs there. We took a pilot on board at the mouth of the estuary to guide us up along the winding waterway.

The cook joined many others, leaning on the railings to watch the mangrove trees and jungle vegetation passing, as well as in the vain hope of seeing native women bathing in the muddy clearings. Then our ship veered a little to one side and the next thing we pressed in against the jungle trees that hung over the river banks. The branches made a whooshing sound as they arched over the deck of our ship.

Then there was a shout of alarm. A black snake about two yards long, apparently resting on a branch, fell off and down on top of our fellows. He was quickly killed with mops and brushes.

However he had sunk his fangs into the forearm of our cook. The poor man was distraught as the punctured flesh began to swell. The Captain came into the radio room and ordered me to send a telegram to the shipping agents, telling them to have medical attention ready as soon as we arrived.

The cook, face white with anxiety, fearing that his end was near, was taken away to hospital in an ambulance. He had to undergo some rigorous treatment to counter the effects of the venom, but he was released after twenty-four hours.

When he returned to our ship his whole being radiated relief. The doctors had given him several bottles of an antivenom solution, a dosage to be taken daily. He was warned that on no account was he to consume alcohol if he valued his health or his life.

From that day on he never touched a drop. He was gradually transformed. He had the cheer of a person who had escaped after a brush with death. Then he began to apply himself to his duties in the kitchen. There was a marked improvement in the food. Meat was properly cooked and well presented. It was appetising. Now we looked forward to meal times. To the surprise of all he proved to be an excellent baker and produced some delicious puddings and sweets.

People came round to watch his performance in the galley, where he moved about with the agility of a ballet dancer, handling deftly the pots and pans and various implements.

By the time we got to the Bay of Biscay his stature and standing on board was high. His checkered aprons were now always spotless and his wispy hair no longer fell forward over his nose.

It was heartening to see a man rejuvenated, taking control of his life. I went out of my way to thank him for the good food he was serving up.

He responded by saying it would be even better but for the fact that the store room was a complete shambles. "That's what happens when the Chief Steward is a piss-artist."

There was one exception to the chorus of praise for our cook. The Chief Engineer still nursed his distaste. "It's a pity he wasn't bitten by a snake at the start of the voyage," he said.

17

FLYING FISH TO THE RESCUE

Salvation for shiwrecked sailors

On my first voyage in the Indian Ocean I was fascinated by the sight of fish breaking the surface of the water, rising above the waves and then gliding along gracefully for long, long distances before splashing into the sea again.

The grizzled Chief Officer, who had been knocking around tropic seas for decades, told me that they were flying fish. They measured about 12 inches (30 centimetres). He said that they had long, wide pectoral fins that could be spread like wings to give them lift as they flew along over the surface of the waves.

They live on plankton. They themselves make a tasty meal for dolphins and porpoises, tuna, marlin, squids and other predators. They escape by vibrating their tails at great speed to give them the thrust for a powerful self-propelled leap into the air.

The long fins, comparable to the shape of a bird's wing, enable them to use the updrafts created by the wind and wave. They can stay above water for water for 30 seconds or more, travelling at speeds estimated at 70 kilometres an hour, covering long distances at heights of up to four or five metres.

They're considered a delicacy in many parts of the tropics and are fished by a variety of methods.

In Zanzibar I got talking to an old Arab sailor who said they sometimes landed on the decks of the dhows that sailed between Arabia and East Africa.

I heard an extraordinary story about flying fish from a man call Rui Mascarenas, who came from the then Portuguese colony of Goa. His father was a steward aboard a cargo ship that was torpedoed in the Indian Ocean in 1942 by a Japanese submarine. He and eight or nine of the Indian crew managed to scramble into the last lifeboat just as the vessel started to go down.

Rough seas had scattered the other lifeboats and in the morning they found themselves alone on the wide open sea. They were badly shaken. Two had been injured by the explosion.

Fortunately, Rui's father and the ship's cook, a resourceful fellow from Gujerat, had managed to lug on board a gunny sack that held a small bag of flour, some lentils and onions as well as a primus stove and some methylated spirits.

They set about providing food for the famished men. They got the primus going, mixed rainwater with the flour and using a plate and rolling-pin made a basic kind of chapati or roti. These were simply small, thin pancakes. But with a sprinkling of lentils and onions they provided some sustenance. More than that it boosted the morale of the distressed men. They raised the sail.

It beame clear that the meagre supply of food would have to be rationed if they were to survive more than six or seven days. Then, on the fifth day, the weakening men, sheltering from the boiling sun under the sail, were startled to find themselve in the path of a shoal of flying fish.

Some thumped onto the deck. Others hit the sail and fell at their feet. The men scrambled about and gathered about a dozen.

The cook prepared these fish and fried some of them on the primus. They were a welcome addition to the chapatis. This fortunate event gave them some hope.

One day later they were overjoyed to see a ship approaching on the horizon. It spotted and rescued them. It was a Greek vessel bound for Cochin on the Malabar coast and it landed them there. Rui's father, relieved to be alive, made his way home to Goa. He was interviewed by a local Portuguese-language newspaper. It ran this remarkable story of survival under the headline *Milagre dos paes e dos peixes* – "Miracle of the loaves and the fishes".

18

READING ULYSSES IN
THE INDIAN OCEAN

Carried back to Dublin from Malabar and Coromandel

One hot afternoon in Colombo, the capital of Sri Lanka, I sought refuge from the boiling tropical sun in a shaded bookshop. There, in one of the long wooden trays, I noticed a big, heavy book with a green hardback cover. Its title was embossed in gold. It was *Ulysses* by James Joyce.

I had heard about this book but I had the impression that it was difficult and tortuous. I took it up hesitantly and began to leaf through it, dipping in here and there. There was a welcome whiff of familiarity about it. The way people spoke, the use of words and phrases, the Dublin setting, the references to things and places that I recognised. There was humour in it as well.

It is said that *Ulysses* is a universal book but it was its Irishness that appealed to me. I bought it because I was homesick. This was in the 1950s. I hadn't been home for almost two years. I was getting tired of sailing about the Indian Ocean on deck-passenger ships on Eastern Service with the Marconi company.

I walked in the heat to the Galle Face hotel that overlooked the sea and went into the Wine Lounge for a long, cold drink. There I began to read *Ulysses*.

After a while, a thin, dark-skinned man appeared beside me. "That is a very strange book. I have read it, even though I don't understand everything in it," he said. I invited him to sit down.

If I remember rightly, Rasaretnam was his name. He told me he had studied medicine in Dublin. There he become familiar with the writings of James Joyce. However, he had failed his exams and his father had called him home. He now ran a small and, according to himself, barely profitable furniture business in Colombo.

When we parted his said, "The more you concentrate on *Ulysses* the more you will enjoy it. It is about everybody." He gave a rueful laugh. "Sometimes I think I am in it too."

I was in an ideal job to give this strange book the kind of attention it needed. I was the second radio officer on a ship called the *Aronda*, plying back and forth every month between Chittagong at the top of the Bay of Bengal and Karachi at the top of the Arabian Sea, stopping at Colombo there and back.

One of the most tiresome duties was the six-hour night watch in the radio room. Little happened. Rarely was a telegram sent or received.

So, sitting there in my shorts, as the ship ploughed steadily through the blackness of the tropic night, I read *Ulysses*. At first I found that a single hour of concentrated reading was all I could manage in one night. It was hard going.

Yet, bit by bit, I began to be fascinated not just by Leopold Bloom, his wife Molly and Stephen Dedalus, but by all the other very real and memorable characters that moved about the streets of Dublin.

Our ship may have been near the coasts of Malabar or Coromandel, but I found myself being carried back to a city I knew fairly well, engrossed in the real-life conversations in its pubs and on street corners. In some ways, reading *Ulysses* was like taking a slow circuitous walk with someone who had an intense interest in the most ordinary things in the lives of ordinary people.

It took me about three months to finish Joyce's masterpiece. When I finally put the book down I had some idea of what Mr Rasaretnam was talking about when he said that *Ulysses* is about everybody.

It's about imperfect, incomplete human beings with whom we can all identify. They endure the dissatisfactions of life with a kind of subdued dignity and occasional humour.

Many of the men in the book, like Leopold Bloom, trudge about the streets trying to make a very uncertain living. Some are just about getting by. For some, the promise of personal fulfilment has faded. One of them might have been Mr Rasaretnam, the failed medical student, now eking out a precarious livelihood in his furniture shop in Colombo.

19

LOVE AND GOSSIP IN THE PERSIAN GULF

Intimate information passing from ship to ship

Some of the women passengers would have been out-raged if they known that information about their ro-mantic inclinations or, more candidly, their "availability", was being passed from one ship to another.

This gossip was being exchanged between the junior ra-dio officers of the four ships of the British India company on what was called the Persian Gulf run. One of these deck-passenger ships left Bombay – now called Mumbai – every week to do the month-long round trip to Basra and back, calling at such ports as Muscat, Dubai, Kuwait, Bandar Ab-bas on the way up and on the way back.

First Class passengers, usually European and mostly British, who lived or worked in those parts, might leave from Bombay, disembark in Dubai or Kuwait for a holiday and then catch a ship heading back.

The philanderers among the officers always kept a weather eye open for unaccompanied women passengers of eligible age. Their hope that that a brief but passionate affair might ensue somewhere between the ports. Among these would-be Casanovas were a few Irish fellows who were Junior Radio Officers.

They hung around the foyer watchfully when passengers were boarding, sizing up the talent. Later, when the ship got under way and a chance presented itself, they would strike up conversations with any attractive woman.

They were aware that some women often lost all inhibitions once they boarded ship. They ate more. They drank more. They flirted. And if some fellow, handsome in his uniform, made easy talk with them, they often felt inclined to have a fleeting fling.

It was greatly to the advantage of these women chasers if they knew which of the women passengers was partial to a swift love affair. That was why, around three in the morning, these fellows on the night watch, would send out a call "Any BI ships around?" There was always one and sometimes two or even three on their way up or down the Persian Gulf.

"Mrs Diana X will be joining you at Kuwait to go back to Bombay. We had her on the way up. The Second Mate had her as well."

"Lovely Welsh bird will be boarding you in Basra to go to Muscat. Bronwen Thomas. She has an interest in Irish literature – but don't pretend you've read *Ulysses* because she's studied it at university. She's very willing."

Like all tittle-tattle, much of it was unreliable and often inaccurate. And it didn't always result in romantic success. I recall overhearing one night an exchange between two of the inveterate womanisers.

"I thought you told me Penelope G. was OK? When I made my move she slapped me down very forcefully."

The response came back quickly. "Ah, you mustn't have the knack. I found her very eager."

I myself was far too shy to be one of these marine Don Juans, but I certainly did take part in such exchanges of idle talk in the small hours of the morning.

I felt a bit uneasy about it until I got talking to a well-seasoned Englishwoman at the Breach Candy swimming club in Bombay. When I told her I was a Radio Officer on the Persian Gulf run she laughed knowingly. "Oh my, there are some very lively Irish fellows on those ships. We know all about them. Some are better than others. A lot of us travel on those ships and we mark one another's cards."

So the traffic in gossip was not just one way.

20

SAILORS ENDING UP IN JAIL – AN OCCUPATIONAL EXPERIENCE

"Don't tell me you've never been behind bars."

We were lying at anchor outside the port city of Santos in Brazil. In the evenings we used to sit around telling yarns.

The subject of spending a night or two in jail came up. This was a fairly common happening for seafarers on ships plying the east coast of South America. The port areas of cities like Santos, Montevideo and Buenos Aires were full of drinking dens, sleazy dance halls, night clubs and strip joints, cabarets and houses of iniquity.

In these throbbing, noisy dives melees often broke out, usually between men who had drunk too much. Even a blameless mariner could find himself in the middle of thumping fists and flying chairs.

Inevitably the police were called. The pugilists were herded outside and into Black Marias. They ended up behind bars. In the morning they were brought before the courts and before judges who were weary of seeing men with black eyes who had broken up the furniture.

Our Chief Officer, a jolly, tubby Englishman, told his story of a night in jail. It happened several years before.

"I was in a night club. A gorgeous pole dancer started performing. I put my drink down to watch. Then I found it in the hand of this greasy fellow. So I biffed him. All hell broke loose. The police arrived and several of us were arrested.

The jail was bedlam. Dreadful place. Chaps snoring and snorting all night. Next morning in court the solicitor for the shipping agents explained what had happened. The judge looked at me and said, through an interpreter: 'Never leave your drink untended in this city. There are two many thirsty fellows around.' I got fined a small sum and was let go."

The Second Officer had his own jail story. As a cadet he was making his way back to the ship in the small hours after a night on the town when he was seized by the need to have a pee. He could find no urinal and in the end relieved himself into a tub of flowers on the promenade. He thought there was nobody about until a police car pulled up and he was taken into custody.

"I was in a cell with a crowd of Swedish sailors who had gone berserk because of drink and had tried to climb the flagpoles outside the presidential palace. Next morning in court I was sentenced to a full day gathering the litter from along the promenade, bottles and beer cans and discarded bags and rubbish of all kinds."

Now it was the turn of the Third Officer. He was a quiet fellow who had a dry sense of humour.

"It was here in Santos in a nightclub. I drank more than my share of the local drink, *caipirinha*. Then all these beautiful girls appeared on the stage and started gyrating. I thought it would be a jolly good idea to join them. Of course the manager hauled me off the stage and I was held by bouncers until the police arrived. I found myself locked up for the night in a sort of cage on my own.

Next morning I was brought before the beak. Our solicitor told the judge that I didn't think I was breaking the law by jumping on to the stage to dance with almost-naked women. The judge had a debauched face with big grey bags under his eyes. He shouted, 'Of course it's against the law. If it wasn't wouldn't we all be doing it.' I got fined."

Then my three shipmates turned towards me. "Well, what's your story about spending a night or two in the clink?"

It was an awkward moment. I was a non-drinker. I was a timid soul who would never get into a row or misbehave. I felt a bit deprived at having to admit that I'd never been arrested and ended up behind bars.

21

TERRIFYING TEMPTATION TO JUMP OVER THE SIDE

It's always there for the disturbed mariner

"All ships, all ships. Man overboard. All ships, all ships. Man overboard in position..."

It's always a chilling appeal for help to hear on the bridge of a ship. If the unfortunate person struggling to stay afloat could possibly be nearby then lookouts are posted. Deck officers and seaman move to the wings of the bridge, scanning the seas with binoculars. In the blackness of the night searchlights can sweep around the sea but it's not too easy, especially if there is any kind of sea running.

Anyone who has gone to sea on a ship or yacht or fishing vessel or any kind of boat knows about the dangers of falling overboard. It's so easy. It happens all too often. There are dangers even on big deep-sea vessels. Seamen working on the lifeboats or near the edge of the deck without railings don't always wear the safety harness they're supposed to.

Then there are people who are distraught of disturbed and fling themselves over the side. Without any doubt the sea flowing past the moving ship can have a sort of mesmeric attraction for anyone who is fed up with life and has an urge to put an end to it.

This happened to me once. I'd been sailing East of Suez for almost three years without a break. My nerves had fallen into a bad state. I had to fight hard to control a trembling hand on the Morse key when sending or receiving messages from coast stations or other ships.

I was the second radio officer on the deck-passenger ship *Sirdhana* and we were heading up the Red Sea to embark Muslim pilgrims who had been to Mecca. We were to take them back to Chittagong at the top of the Bay of Bengal.

The heat was appalling. We had no air conditioning. Day and night the heat pressed down on us relentlessly.

One night when I was keeping my six-hour watch I fled the claustrophobic oven of the radio room, where the heat from the receivers added to the temperature. I wanted to get a breath of air of some kind so I climbed up to the very top open deck over the bridge.

There was nothing but the sky above. It was a night of brilliant moonlight that was reflected on the glittering sea. I stayed there for a while and then edged my way slowly to the side of the open deck. For a moment I looked down at the sea moving past below with the ship's bow wave spreading away. For a split second I had a terrifying impulse to jump and plunge into the waters far below.

I leapt back fearfully. I turned and ran for the companionway. As I went down the steps I clung to the railings with both hands, as if to restrain any mad urge to jump over the side. I abandoned the radio room and sought the sanctuary of my cabin. Not only did I shut the slatted inside door but also the solid outside door, as if to shut out temptation.

Then I lay on my bunk, perspiring in the sweltering heat, slowly calming down.

After a few hours, my morale restored I went back to the radio room. The Chief Radio Officer, Eddie O'Brien from Sandymount in Dublin was there, wondering where I was. I told him of my unnerving experience.

"You've been out East too long," said this decent, kindly man. "You need to be back in Erin's green isle, even if the cold winds are howling and the rain lashing down and the clouds sweeping across the sky. And sitting down to bacon, cabbage and boiled potatoes."

He was right, of course. When we eventually got to Calcutta I told the Marconi Company I'd had enough of Eastern Service. When the *Sirdhana* arrived in Singapore I was relieved and flew home to Ireland, and made my way to Omeath, on the shores of Carlingford Lough.

I felt the change in temperature and shivered. But I was among my sisters and younger brother, and my mother fed me well. When I began walking along the roadway with the Cooley Mountains rearing up all round, my spirits were restored.

22

MEDICAL CARE AND ATTENTION FOR THE SHIP'S DOCTOR

"Nobody was as well cared for."

"Thank the Lord we have a doctor on board," said one of our twelve American passengers as they boarded in New York for a long voyage that would take us across the Pacific Ocean to Australia.

Some were elderly and I suppose it was a source of comfort for them to know that if they fell ill in the middle of nowhere, there was a ship's doctor to hand.

Our cargo ship, of the Ellerman Line, carried 12 passengers. This was in the pre-container era, when the design of cargo ships left some spare accommodation space that the owners wanted to put to profitable use.

Regulations decreed that a doctor must be carried. Many of these seafaring medics were men who found it difficult to settle after they qualified. Some found they were unsuited for the business of doctoring. In the end they took to seafaring as a kind of last resort. Some had an especial fondness for alcohol.

Our Irish doctor was one of these, although he was a decent and genial man. During our crossing of the Atlantic to the US he never touched a drop. However, when we reached the Panama Canal, he received a letter from Ireland telling him that his sister was seriously ill. He was very close to her.

He hit the bottle. We were not a dry ship and he had access to beer and spirits. There was a small passenger bar and our doctor took up his favourite seat there. He was tipsy well before the evening began but nobody took much notice of him. Then he began to interrupt the conversations of others by bawling out songs like *Let Eireann Remember* and *Oft in the Stilly Night*.

His condition became noticeable a day or two later when, at dinner, his wayward elbow knocked his soup onto the lap of a stout lady from North Carolina.

He staggered up the stairs and flopped into his bunk. He seemed unable to rise and remained there for several days. The Captain, a jolly fellow from the Wirral area of Liverpool, visited him and looked him over. The Skipper ordered that no more drink be supplied to him.

We also carried a nurse, a fine woman from Donegal. She looked him over. "The drink has the better of him," she said. She would look after him as best she could.

The poor man lay there on his bunk, a picture of alcoholic misery. Yet for all that, he never lost his sense of humour. His cabin was beside mine and when I dropped in to see him he often quoted from the Bible: "Physician, heal thyself."

One of our passengers was a just-retired doctor. He was a hearty, cheerful fellow. The day he boarded he said with a laugh, "I hope I've examined my very last patient." The

Captain now approached him and asked him, as a favour, to look at his distressed fellow medic. He did so.

"He'll be OK. I've seen worse," said the American. "But he's got to be kept off the booze. I'll call to see him a few times a day." He recommended nutritious broths and the Chief Steward provided these.

"How's our doctor coming along?" the passengers used ask every day.

Gradually, as our ship moved across the vast empty reaches of the Pacific, our doctor slowly regained his health. He certainly got plenty of attention – from the Captain, the US doctor, the Nurse, the Chief Steward and others like myself.

He rose, shakily at first, and stepped about. It took some courage on his part to eventually make his way down to the promenade deck and to the saloon. When the passengers caught sight of him they clapped. He smiled, a bit embarrassed.

By the time the coast of Australia appeared on the far horizon our doctor was in fine fettle. The Captain, with a faint grin, said to me, "It's good to know that if any of us had fallen sick, we had our very own ship's doctor on board to look after us."

23

THE GREAT SEA BATTLE
OF LEPANTO

Both sides claimed Divine support

October 7 is the anniversary of one of the most decisive and significant naval battles in history. This was the battle of Lepanto, off the western coast of Greece. It took place in the year 1571. This was the last major naval engagement fought almost entirely by galleys, where men pulled on oars.

It involved some 600 ships and 140,000 soldiers, oarsmen and crews. The galleys of the Holy League, an alliance of Catholic states led by Spain and Venice, confronted those of the Ottoman Turks, the dominant power in the Eastern Mediterrenan whose capital was Istanbul.

The long heavy oars, sometimes in two tiers, were mostly pulled by captives, slaves or convicts shackled to the wooden seats. They kept stroke to the loud, dominating beat of the timekeeper's drum. Overseers wielded whips with which to lash anyone they thought was not pulling his weight.

This battle for supremacy of the Mediterranean had been in the offing for many years. The fast, skilfully-guided galleys of rhe Turks had proven superior to those of the Christians in numerous encounters. The capture of the key island of Cyprus signalled the intention of the Ottomans to move further west into the Mediterranean. Their war-galleys were now threatening the coasts of Italy, Sardinia and even the cities of Venice and Rome.

The various powers of the Holy League were compelled to put aside their rivalries, jealousies and suspicions and assemble a fleet to confront the Turks. Commanded by Don Juan of Austria, the naval force moved slowly towards Lepanto where the Ottoman fleet was anchored.

The Turks, under the astute and courageous Ali Pasha, responded to the challenge. During the morning the two fleets, each spread in a line of battle across a distance of four miles, rowed slowly towards one another. The sea was relatively calm. Both Christians and Muslims claimed to have God on their side and each flew banners of religious significance.

The Ottomans had 280 galleys as against 170 for the Holy League. However. Don Juan's ships had greater fire-power in the form of cannons and other artillery. In addition, the Venetians had provided six large merchant vessels that had been converted into heavily gunned warships.

The two battle fleets closed on one another. When they were only 150 yards apart the gunners put their lighted tapers to the cannons. A deafening roar filled the air. The superior fire-power of the Holy League was immediately evident as cannon balls smashed into the wood of the Ottoman galleys.

Like enemy chieftains in combat, the big galleys of Don Juan and Ali Pasha smashed into one another, pouring hundreds of soldiers into face-to-face fighting on the decks as each tried to take possession of the rival ship. This was repeated all along the line. Musket balls and arrows felled hundreds of combatants as the galleys thumped into one another and soldiers jumped aboard. Men hacked at one another with swords and pikes on decks that ran with blood. The slaughter was appalling.

Gradually, many of the Turkish ships were overcome. But they were hardened battlers and they fought on to the bitter end. The carnage and turmoil lasted four hours before the Holy League emerged victorious.

When the battle eventually ended the sea was filled with bodies, smashed oars, yardarms, casks and burning ships. More than 40,000 men were dead, 25,000 from the Ottoman ranks. This was killing on a huge scale. Witnesses were horrified by the sight of the bloodbath.

The battle of Lepanto dented Turkish power and it ended the threat of invasion of Italy and Spain. Eventually, France and Venice made peace with the Ottomans.

Oar-powered galleys had been used in naval combat since Greek and Roman times, but the battle of Lepanto marked a turning point. Galleys were too vulnerable to the kind of greatly improved and effective gunnery that had won the day. From then on, the emphasis was to be on naval fire-power.

24

SCATTERING CAPTAIN'S ASHES IN THE ARABIAN SEA

The Merry Widow enlivened the bar

On one of my first voyages we scattered the ashes of a former ship's Captain. He had spent most of his life sailing about the Indian Ocean. His dying request in hospital in Bombay was that his ashes be scattered in the middle of the Arabian Sea.

Our ship plied back and forth between India and East Africa so it was decided that this solemn ceremony should take place on our way to Mombasa. His wife, who was at least twenty years younger, was to sail with us to attend the commemoration.

Our Captain was anxious that everything be done properly. He assigned our Senior Cadet, a personable, handsome fellow of 18 called Derek, to go to the widow's apartment on Malabar Hill to collect the ashes and take them on board. The urn was then kept under lock and key in the Captain's cabin.

Derek also collected the widow and her baggage in one of the company cars and saw her safely on board. She was given one of the better First Class cabins. She was put sitting at the Captain's table.

Widow she may have been but she cut a glamorous figure. She was a beautiful woman. Not only that but, surprisingly, she was vivacious and full of humour. She didn't at all seem like someone consumed by grief.

As a Junior Radio Officer I kept the six-hour night-time watch. If nothing was happening on the air waves I often went up to the bridge to chat to the Second Officer.

Derek kept watch with him. One of his duties was to do the rounds of our deck-passenger ship every hour to ensure all was in order. On our second night at sea he reported that the widow was still in the First Class bar at 1.00 a.m. and a bit unsteady on her feet.

The Second Mate ordered him to go down and make sure she got safely to her cabin. He said, "The last thing we want is for the Merry Widow to be at the ash-scattering ceremony with a bandage round her head like a turban." Much the same thing happened the following nights.

One afternoon when we were about midway through the voyage we assembled on the promenade deck in our white tropical uniforms. The Captain carried the urn from his cabin and went to the railings. The Merry Widow stood beside him.

There was a light breeze that would blow the ashes away out to sea. However, high-sided ships can cause wind-flurries that defy the general wind direction. When the Captain shook the ashes over the side they were caught by an updraft of eddying wind and actually came back over the deck like a grey whirling ghost. The embarrassing moment was broken when the Merry Widow piped up with a radiant smile, "My husband was always an awkward sort of chap."

Fortunately, just then a gust of wind blew the ashes away out to sea.

Until the end of the voyage she was the life and soul of drinking sessions in the bar. And each night Derek went down to ensure she reached her cabin without mishap.

When we came alongside at Mombasa there was a crowd of friends waiting for her, to whisk her away to Nairobi.

That evening the Second Mate came into my cabin for a chat and a drink. He told me that the second night Derek had helped the Merry Widow to her cabin she had flung herself on him. despite the difference in age.

"I don't think our Derek showed much reluctance. In fact, I think he was rather eager. He was away for an hour or so every night. It's a good sign for his career, being concerned to look after the needs of passengers."

25

COURAGE AND DUTY AT SEA

Themes in the novels of Józef Conrad

The courage and composure of those at sea is tested at times of danger. When the vessel begins to list in heavy seas. When it springs a leak. When a serious fire breaks out in the engine-room. When the vessel shudders and groans as it crunches onto rocks. These are the events when seafarers have to be as brave as they can. They have to act as resolutely and calmly as possible. Their own lives or those of passengers may be at risk.

Others have to risk their lives too. The crews of the lifeboats and rescue helicopters and other vessels that come to the aid of the distressed put their lives in danger, especially in stormy seas. They answer the call of duty.

The obligation to put the lives of others above their own comes to the fore on passenger ships. The Captain, officers and crew are obliged to risk their own survival in order to save the lives of passengers.

These themes of courage and duty at sea are interwoven into some of the novels of Józef Conrad, the Polish writer who settled in England and wrote in English.

He spent some twenty years at sea between 1873 and 1894. He sailed in the French and British merchant navies and attained a Master's Certificate. He experienced all the dangers of seafaring.

Conrad developed sharp insights into the human condition. He knew that mariners, like everyone else, were fallible human beings. At times of crisis they didn't always measure up to their ideals. They weren't always brave. They didn't always do their duty.

In one of his novels, *Lord Jim*, published in 1900, Conrad tells the story of how a man was haunted by an incident of human weakness in his seafaring life. Jim was Mate on a ship called the *Patna*, carrying Muslim pilgrims going to the holy city of Mecca. However, when the vessel struck a reef, Jim followed the Captain and white officers who hurried into a lifeboat, abandoning the distraught passengers to their fate.

Jim and his accomplices were rescued by another ship. However, the *Patna* did not sink and was towed into port. In the official enquiry that followed Jim was denounced for dereliction of duty; his Mate's Certificate was taken from him. For the rest of his life this basically decent man was deeply troubled by this incidence of weakness.

The story of *Lord Jim* is said to be based on a real event. A British ship, the *Jeddah*, carrying almost 1,000 pilgrims, got into difficulties in the Red Sea in the year 1880. The hull sprung a leak and the water began to rise rapidly. The Captain and officers abandoned both ship and its Asian passengers and jumped into a lifeboat. They were picked up by another ship and taken to the port of Aden. There they told the port authorities a story about the passengers becoming dangerously violent amidst the most appalling panic. They said they had no option but to scramble to safety.

Then, to their astonishment and perhaps dismay, a French ship towed the *Jeddah* into the harbour. All the pilgrims had survived. An official enquiry followed, as it does in Conrad's novel, where the captain and officers were roundly condemned.

I first came across that book in a ship's library and was fascinated by this nautical tale of human frailty. I was reading the book in the radio room when the Captain came in. He took it up.

"Yeah, I've read that book," he said. "We all hope that if something goes wrong, if we go on the rocks or the ship takes fire or whatever, that we'll hold our nerve, that we won't panic. It doesn't always happen. We can't be certain. We just hope that we'll have the courage to do whatever it takes."

26

ALBERT THE ALBATROSS

Followed us faithfully for three days

The Second Mate shouted into my cabin: "Come on, if you want to see a sight. We have a mighty albatross following in our wake."

I'd never seen an albatross before and hurried down with him to the stern railings. About fifty yards behind us, this enormous bird glided effortlessly over the dark blue waves.

We had a strong following wind and sea and the albatross was using the conditions with astonishing mastery. We watched it skimming up the waves and then floating downwards into the troughs. Sometimes it veered off to one side but, without flapping its wings, it returned to a position astern.

It was strange to realise that this big bird was following us, keeping pace with us using wind and wave so skillfully.

"They can follow ships for days," said the Second Mate, who had made a study of these marine birds.

Our vessel, the *Icenic* of the Shaw Savill line, was on her way from Perth to Melbourne, voyaging along the upper edge of the Southern Ocean, where these largest of marine birds can be seen.

Later, in his cabin, he showed me a big illustrated book about them. He told me that their wingspan could reach 12 feet or 3 metres. Not only that but they were able to lock those mighty wings into the outspread position so that no muscular energy was needed to control them.

"They can travel 800 or 900 miles at a time without much effort," he told me.

This huge bird has a long hooked bill, with sharp edges. It feeds on fish, squid, and krill, often scooping them up while in flight.

The albatross has fascinated sailors and explorers over the centuries. There was a belief that harming an albatross would bring bad luck if not disaster. The Second Mate was able to recite verses of the *Rime of the Ancient Mariner* by Samuel Taylor Coleridge. In this poem a sailor kills an albatross and is punished by having the dead bird strung around his neck. This led to the saying, "having an albatross around your neck", for someone carrying a heavy burden, or having to endure a crushing disadvantage.

Ever so often during daylight hours we went down to the stern to look at what we were calling "our albatross". There was always one or two of the crew leaning on the railings, watching. Someone had christened it Albert. It was fascinating to see it coasting along over the waves so gracefully, floating on air but well able to keep up with a ship doing 25 knots or more.

Albert followed us faithfully for three days.

Then, on the morning of the fourth day it could not be seen anywhere. The Second Mate and I stood at the stern for a long time, scanning the dark rolling waves of that ocean.

"Well, that's it, Albert's gone," he said.

We felt just a little sad that this big bird had left us. We had developed a sort of affection for it.

Seafaring lore said that albatrosses were the souls of lost sailors, and indeed many men perished in the vast turbulent sea that is the Southern Ocean. Maybe such beliefs, however far-fetched, gave seafarers a special interest in this huge bird.

27

SAILOR ON HORSEBACK WITH NATIONAL HEROES

Story behind lop-sided nose

The nose of our genial Third Officer was a bit out of kilter. He himself used say, "Oh, it has a distinct westward slant."

His was a most unusual story. This tall sinewy fellow came from a family of distinguished landowners. They were well-known for horse riding, foxhunting, eventing and show jumping.

He told me he was an accomplished horseman who had ambitions. However there were some unfortunate incidents that blighted his prospects.

"I had this irresistible impulse to cut corners, take short cuts, when I was competing at cross-country events," he said. Some quirky gremlin in his personality kept tempting him to cheat, which he frequently did. Inevitably, he was caught and suspended from further competitions. He was only sixteen at the time and the incident cast a cloud over his equestrian aspirations.

His family, who hobnobbed with royalty and the aristocracy, were very embarrassed. They were even more upset

84

when, during a hunt ball, he was discovered in the garden astride the wife of the Master of the Hounds, a weathered lady much older than he.

These misdeeds decided his fate. His family decided that to atone for them he should be packed off to sea as a Deck Cadet. He joined the Royal Mail shipping company, whose vessels plied between South America and the UK.

He soon found himself walking the streets of ports like Recife, Santos, Rio de Janeiro, Porto Alegre, Montivideo and Buenos Aires.

"I was immediately struck by the number of public monuments of chaps mounted on horseback. In every city there were fellows seated on chargers, brandishing swords, pointing the way forward."

These equine monuments commemorated national heroes who had fought to liberate their countries from Spanish rule back in the 1800s. There were statues of Simón Bolívar in many cities in Brazil. In Argentina, the national liberator, José de San Martín, looked down from his noble steed. In Chile, Bernardo O'Higgins, whose father came from County Sligo, surveyed passersby on the plaza from his vantage point.

Our Third Officer told me that one night he was heading back on board after drinking quite a bit when he came on one of these monuments near the waterfront.

"I was seized by an impulse to climb up behind the horseman. It game me an enormous thrill, sitting high over the esplanade, as if San Martín regarded me as a trusted lieutenant and told me to hop up behind."

After that he regularly indulged this unusual whim after a night on the town. He soon found that doing so carried risks. One night in Porto Alegre, he was stopped from sitting up behind some mounted hero by a group of angry citizens who threatened to call the police. On another occasion the police actually arrived and he had to dismount hurriedly and scurry down alleyways to avoid arrest. It was a chancy business.

"In the end I decided to call it a day after I had made one final climb. Our ship was in Buenos Aires and I chose the statue of Simón Bolívar in the Rivadavia Park."

Somewhat under the weather, he went there in the small hours with another cadet who had a flash camera. There were few people around. While his accomplice kept watch he vaunted over the surrounding flower beds and hopped on the white pedestal.

"I grabbed hold of the horse's tail, climbed up one of his legs and then sat astride the horse behind Bolívar, who has his sword held aloft. My fried took a photo of me and I was delighted."

Unfortunately, on the way back down he slipped and bashed his nose. His friend called an ambulance and he was taken to a nearby hospital.

"They made a bad job of it," he said.

When he got back to England his uncle met him at the station and asked what had happened to his nose.

"I got it when I toppled off a horse," he replied, without going into any detail.

His uncle, a former show jumper, said: "Oh jolly good. If one has to get a lop-sided nose it's best to get it falling off a horse."

28

THE SUN BREAKS THROUGH AT LONG LAST

"I thought I'd never see the bloody thing again."

One of the great experiences of seafaring is when, after long, exhausting days of gales and turbulent seas, the ship reaches a latitude where the weather changes for the better.

Nothing raises the spirits as much as the glorious vision of bright, warm sunshine after days of dreary, storm-torn clouds. And the longer people have had to endure heaving decks, rain and dark skies, the greater the delight when the sun finally comes through.

That happened on a small cargo ship I once sailed on. We had crossed the North Atlantic in mid-winter and had to put up with over 14 days of storms. The seas broke over the prow. A sodden mattress of cloud rolled by overhead day after day. We thought that once we had reached New York the weather might change. The only change was that it got bitterly cold.

The dreary grey weather was still there after we left, bound for the Gulf of Mexico. We were three days sailing south and still the sun was nowhere to be seen. The seas were not quite as heavy but they were unpleasantly choppy and the air still cool.

"Will we ever see the blasted sun again?" said the Third Mate, after yet another shower of rain swept the decks. Bad weather had kept everybody indoors most of the time for weeks on end, resting in their cabins after they came off watch.

But the following day there was a marvellous transformation. In the afternoon the waves began to subside, losing their rough bustle. A balmy breeze replaced the irritating, flapping wind. The cloud cover overhead began to lighten, brightened by yellow sunlight. I went up to the bridge and stood on the wing with the Third Mate, sensing the change.

Then, like an oasis in the desert, we saw a patch of blue sky far ahead. It got bigger and bigger. The sea below it sparkled with sunlight. Within an hour the thin cloud cover had dissolved into little cotton balls that floated tranquilly beneath the vast blue heavens.

Now the sun, warm and benign, began to dry the wooden deck timbers. It glistened on the railings. It heated the iron deck-plates around the holds. It turned the canvas hatch covers a light, dry grey. A smell of iron, of warmed wood, of sea-salt began to waft about our sea-battered ship.

This sea-change aroused a great uplifting of spirits. Men came out on deck in singlets and trousers, stretching and yawning. They blinked in the strong yellow light. They patted their bare arms as if to assure themselves that the sun was actually shining on them. They were like cave-dwellers who had retreated to the darkest places to escape a storm, but who now came forward into the bright, warm air.

Men smiled easily, walked about with a lighter step. Some began to hum and others puckered up their lips to whistle awkwardly. Portholes that had been tightly clamped for weeks were unscrewed and prised open energetically. A stream of warm fresh air ran through the ship, sweeping away sour cooking smells and the musty odour of damp clothing.

The Third Mate and I raised our faces towards the sun. Its warm rays soothed the skin around our eyes that for so long had been crinkled against gale, sleet and rain. It had an exhilarating effect. We felt on good terms with the sea and with life.

Trying to sound wise, I said, "Well, I suppose we'll get tired of the sun after a few weeks of it." He turned to me and said, "Listen to me – after what we've been through, it will take a long, long time before I get fed up with sunshine."

29

TRAGEDY OFF THE COAST OF BRAZIL

Panic and confusion led to much loss of life

Our ship, the *Drina*, was off the coast of Brazil bound for Rio de Janiero.

The Captain tapped his pencil on the chart where an icon indicated a sunken shipwreck.

"That's the wreck of the Italian passenger liner, the *Principessa Mafalda*. A total fiasco. Panic and mayhem. Crew ran amok. People drowned that should have been saved."

The disaster of this transatlantic liner, once the flagship of Italy's leading shipping company, made world headlines in 1927. She went down with the loss of 314 out of 1,250 passengers and crew. It remains the greatest marine tragedy in Italian peace-time shipping.

She was launched in 1910 and named after Princess Mafalda, the second daughter of the Italian monarch, Victor Emmanuel III.

The vessel, of 9,200 tons, was designed for the voyage between Genoa and Buenos Aires. She became known for her luxury, spacious First Class cabins, two-story ballroom

90

and excellent food. However, after many years voyaging on the route she became prone to mechanical faults. The liner was now spoken of as trailing faded grandeur in her wake.

In 1927 she set off on one more voyage. It soon became apparent that this imposing old vessel was only creaking along. Several times she stopped in mid-ocean while the engineers struggled with the engines. The failure of a refrigeration system resulted in food becoming contaminated; there were cases of food poisoning.

At the Cape Verde islands stop the liner was supplied with fresh food. Some repairs were carried out and it continued on its journey. It seemed that all was well. The ship crossed the Equator with a colourful ceremony, the orchestra playing and an enormous cake produced by the team of chefs.

However by 23 October, it had developed a list to port, although travelling at full speed. Two days later, 80 miles off Salvador de Bahia in Brazil, there came a great trembling. The starboard propeller shaft had fractured. It had shifted off its axis and gouged several gashes in the hull. It was found that the watertight doors could not be closed.

The Captain had an SOS sent out and very shortly afterwards several ships came to the rescue, including a Dutch and a British liner. With clear weather and ships standing by it seemed that the crisis was under control.

However, panic spread like wildfire on board. Not all the lifeboats could be launched due to the pronounced list of the ship. Some were rushed and swamped by frantic passengers. One of the first lifeboats to get safely away was filled almost entirely with crew, including the ship's Purser, a very senior figure. Other lifeboats making their escape had many crew members on board, while passengers yelled from the railings of the sinking ship.

Confusion and even gunfire on the *Principessa Mafalda*, as well as confusing messages, made it difficult for the rescuing ships to provide effective help. They launched lifeboats and picked up many from the sea.

Amid final scenes of utter chaos, the Captain drowned and the Chief Engineer was reported to have shot himself. The liner sank stern first.

Some months later there was an official enquiry. However the behaviour of the crew was not dealt with. Maybe the Italian government was embarrassed by their conduct.

A sad echo to the tragedy was the fate of Princess Mafalda, after whom the ship was named. Married to a German prince, her attitude towards the Nazi regime aroused the hatred of Adolf Hitler. Near the end of World War Two she was arrested by the Gestapo and died in Buchenwald concentration camp.

There are several memorials to her and some years ago she was commemorated on an Italian postage stamp.

As far as I know, there is no memorial to the ship that bore her name apart from that small icon on marine charts showing where she went down.

30

"ARRIVAL AT TWELVE TONS OR THEREABOUTS"

Enigma of a coded message

The Captain of our deck-passenger ship that plied be-tween Bombay and East Africa had a worried, peevish air about him. He sometimes complained to his officers about this and that in a slow, dry, upper-class English accent.

His white tropical uniform shorts and shirt emphasised his fatness. His knees and arms were a boiled red colour from a lifetime sailing East of Suez.

My boss, the Chief Radio Officer hated him. They were at loggerheads over a series of events. On leaving Bombay our ship sailed up the coast to the Gulf of Kutch, a wide inlet of the sea in the province of Gujerat. It is shallow and notorious for its high tides and shifting sands.

We were anchoring off the port of Bedi Bunder to pick up cargo and passengers. On the bridge deck the echo sounder was churning away. On a roll of electrolytic paper it showed the depth of water beneath our keel. Our Captain consulted it often and so did the deck officers.

Then it ran out of paper. The Captain immediately sent for the Chief R/O. He went up from the radio room and looked in the small press beside the echo sounder. It was empty. The Captain was furious. "You should have checked before we sailed, Sparks." The Chief slunk away.

"We're out of shit-house paper," he said and ordered me to undertake a thorough check on all the spare parts and accessories we were meant to carry.

There was another incident about three days later. The Chief went down to the promenade deck to chat up some woman passenger he had his eye on. Some young Indian girls were playing deck quoits nearby. When one of the small rope rings came flying along the deck and under the feet of the Chief he got annoyed. Unfortunately, like some Irish, he had adopted the racial attitudes of some of the remnants of the British Raj, and he shouted some rude remarks at the girls.

Their mother was outraged. She complained to the Purser and the Captain got to hear of it. He insisted that the Chief apologise to the woman and her youngsters. It was a bit of a humiliation for him.

"That fat slug has it in for me," he said. Then he warned me, "Don't give him any excuse to criticise us."

Actually the Captain never acknowledged my presence even when I delivered the weather forecast to the bridge. He wasn't given to friendly greetings, especially to a Trainee Radio Officer on his first trip.

There was actually another incident on our voyage back from East Africa. The Chief went down to the bar each evening to quaff gin and tonics and keep an eye out for any woman passenger who might be open to a shipboard romance. One evening, his judgement clouded by drink, he placed his hand above the knee of a Scottish woman. She recoiled and later complained to the Captain. Once again he castigated the Chief for unseemly behaviour and ordered him to apologise to the woman.

The Chief, afire with rage and resentment, again warned me, unnecessarily, "Watch your step with him."

Then, when we were about three days away from Bombay, there was an incident that certainly did concern me and the Chief as well. When I went on the night watch at midnight I heard Bombay Radio sending out the four-letter call-sign of our ship. He had a telegram for us. I hesitated about answering his call because I found my competence in Morse to be shaky.

I went round to the Chief's cabin. The light was off and he was fast asleep, sprawled on his settee on his back, clad only in his underpants. His dentures were out and his mouth a sunken hole that gave an echoing sound to his snoring. I made a few weak attempts to wake him but he was out for the count.

When I went back to the radio room I decided to call Bombay, went on a working frequency and copied down the telegram. It was for the Captain. I was uneasy when I found the text was in five-letter commercial code. However I put it in an envelope and delivered it to the bridge.

Next morning there was a fuss. The Captain was mystified by a group of letters that decoded as, "arrival at twelve tons or thereabouts". The Chief was called up to the Captain's cabin. When he came down he switched on the transmitter. With his mouth tight with anger, he hammered on the Morse key with his nail-bitten fingers, calling Bombay and getting them to repeat the telegram. It turned out that I had got one single letter wrong. He went quickly back to the Captain. The text now made commercial sense, related to our sacks of cloves from Zanzibar.

The Chief in his sharp Belfast accent and sharper tongue berated me. Later he said, "Sorry if I was a wee bit harsh but that man is always looking for things to complain about."

I felt a bit downcast. It didn't help that the words "arrival at twelve tons or thereabout" became a source of amusement to the deck officers.

Then, when we were almost in sight of the Indian coast, I was sitting in the radio room when the Captain appeared at the door. There was just a faint glimmer of friendliness on his red face. In his weary tones he said: "Look Sparks, this is all new to you. We all make mistakes. Don't worry about it." Before I could utter a word in response he had gone.

Some months later he announced that he would be leaving our ship because of heart problems.

The Chief was delighted with this news. "No wonder his ticker is packing up. He wore himself out whining and whinging."

I wasn't going to get into an argument with him, but to myself I said, "He had some good points as well."

31

"DOCTOR MASSAGE" AND HIS SPECIAL SKILLS

"I must do a crash-course in this massage business."

Our doctor was a small, sallow-faced, soft-spoken man, a member of the Parsi community from Gujerat, now resident in Bombay. Although only in his mid-thirties he was completely bald.

He had big, round, brown eyes that gave him a soulful look but that somehow evoked trust in anyone who needed his attention.

Some of the British officers on our deck-passenger ship that went to and fro between India and East Africa referred to him as "Doctor Massage." He had a well-deserved reputation for his skill in alleviating, if not completely curing, the pain and discomfort of strains in muscles and tendons.

Not long after I joined the ship I hobbled into his surgery, bent double. I had wrenched a muscle in my back while heaving shut the heavy door of the radar hut.

"Don't worry. I am putting that right," he said. He told me that he had developed a massage treatment that combined the best traditions of the Indian sub-continent.

97

"It is restoring pulled muscles and also encouraging them to loosen up and to relax."

There was something about his modest manner that gave me confidence in his ability as I lay on the table in the surgery. On the palms of his hands he poured a liniment from a small brown earthenware bottle. It smelt of sandalwood and exotic herbs. Then he began to gently knead this balm into the pulled muscle in my back.

After ten minutes it felt less painful. Another ten minutes and even the soreness had disappeared. I walked out of there more or less cured.

Three or four days later out ship pulled away from Ballard Pier with several deep growling blares of its siren and set off for East Africa.

Among our First Class passengers was a beautiful Indian actress, the star of many popular films. Apparently she was going Mombasa, Dar es Salaam and on to Nairobi to promote her films and the Indian film industry among the large Indian population in the region. As far as I remember, Air India flew a route from Bombay to Nairobi via Aden, but she chose the seven-day voyage on our ship.

She was not alone but had a companion/secretary of her own age, though not quite as beautiful. In their scintillating silk saris, with bare, light-brown midriffs, they drew a lot of attention.

The ship's Purser told me she had discarded her husband and was known to have had a number of affairs with male film stars.

The Third Mate and I went down to the promenade deck one afternoon with the intention of exploring out chances with these Oriental beauties. We greeted them and tried to make small talk, but we were like gawky adolescents in the presence of radiant glamour. We backed away gracelessly. However, later on I noticed Doctor Massage sitting with the two, totally at his ease, chatting amiably, sometimes laughing.

Every night, after he had finished his watch at midnight, the Third Officer did the rounds of the ship to ensure nothing was amiss. At the end of his tour he usually dropped into the radio room where I was keeping the six-hour night watch.

One night he entered, grinning. "I've just seen the Movie Queen slipping into Doctor Massage's cabin."

Two night later, this time keeping his eyes well peeled, he had again seen her gliding gracefully into the doctor's cabin.

When I bumped into our doctor the next day I winked at him knowingly and said, "I think you've become very friendly with that film star."

But he held up his hand and shook his head. "No, no. It is simply that she is finding it hard to sleep. The heat, the noise of the engines, the swaying of the ship. It is making her stressed. I am massaging her neck and her shoulders to help her relax. Then she goes back to her cabin and she is sleeping."

I accepted his explanation.

Then our ship reached Mombasa. On the dockside below there was a party of Indian well-wishers to meet her, with several cars waiting to whisk the Movie Queen and her companion away. The Third Mate and I stood at the railings of the promenade deck to watch her going down the gangway. At the bottom she turned around, looked up and waved up. I waved back.

"She's not waving at you, for God's sake," said the Third Mate. "She's waving at Doctor Massage standing right above us on the boar deck."

He told me that on our last night at sea curiosity got the better of him. He sneaked along the passage-way down to the doctor's cabin. Raising himself on his toes he peeped in through the slatted wooden door. He saw Doctor Massage and the Movie Queen entwined on the settee, making vigorous love.

He said, "If that's one of the benefits of this Indian massage treatment, then I'm anxious to do a crash course at first opportunity."

32

MYSTERY OF EAGLE THAT LANDED ON OUR SHIP

Visitor from the high reaches of the Zagros Mountains

A most unusual thing occurred while our ship was at anchor off the port of Bandar Abbas on the southern coast of Iran. The Captain and I were in the chartroom, looking down at the chart of the Persian Gulf, when one of the Indian seamen ran in.

"Captain sahib, a big bird is coming on this ship," he shouted.

We went out to find a large bird perched on the wing of the bridge. It had fierce-looking yellow eyes and a curved beak that looked sharp as a razor. It gripped the wooden rail with large talons. It's breast was a greyish colour, its wings a speckled brown

"It's an eagle," the Captain said. "I've seen many of them years ago when I was trekking in the Zagros Mountains."

These mountains were not too far away, rearing up to high peaks, blue in the midday heat. "It's a total mystery why it should leave its natural habitat and fly out here to sea," he said.

When half an hour went by and this impressive bird was still perched there we wondered if it was injured. Then it began to flap its wings and moved a few steps along the rail.

"Maybe it's just hungry," said the Captain. He ordered one of the Goan stewards to go down to the galley for some minced meat.

The man came back with saucers of meat and water. He laid these cautiously on the wooden deck. The eagle looked down on them and, after five minutes or so, flapped its wings and jumped down. It ate quickly, head jerking forward, sharp beak thrusting into the meat. Then it turned and put its beak into the water.

"It seems OK, doesn't look injured," said the Captain. He told us that the shepherds in the Zagros Mountains had said that eagles sometimes pounced on new-born lambs, grasped them in their strong talons and carried them away to devour. The men sometimes fired shots to scare the birds away and some laid poison.

Our Captain knew something of this great mountain range that stretches from Iraq down the length of Iran. During an extended leave, when he was a cadet, he had backpacked his way alone there. He spent two months walking along the heights and valleys, absorbed in the flora and fauna but especially birds. He learned enough Persian to be able to chat to the shepherds. He often camped with them at night.

"That was a great adventure," he often said. "The trouble was that it made me regret not going on to university instead of going to sea."

Growing up in rural England, he had developed an intense interest in birds, in wildlife, in flowers. He had wanted to study for a degree in botany or the study of birds and wild creatures. He was very disappointed that family finances didn't allow that and he went on for a career at sea instead.

The eagle stayed on the bridge for about an hour. Then it suddenly flapped its wings and flew away, all the time gaining height. With strong, heavy wing-beats it flew high over the city and towards the mountains.

The Captain kept watching it through the binoculars. "It's gone and good luck to it," he said.

On our way up the coast to Bushire the Zagros Mountains were always in view. Very often the Captain would stand on the wing, scanning them with his binoculars. I don't think he expected to spot any eagles but I wondered if he was thinking of the memorable trek he had made there as a young man. I wondered too if he still lamented turning away from a career studying wildlife and flowers, instead of spending most of his life sailing about the Indian Ocean, the Persian Gulf and the China Seas.

33

THE REVENGE OF
THE PRESS BARON

Campaign of vilification
following Titanic disaster

Many stories and incidents surround the tragedy of the *Titanic* and its aftermath. One is a tale of undying enmity and malice. A poisonous ill-will was directed at Bruce Ismay, the Chairman of the White Star Line, by the US press baron, William Randolph Hearst.

Ismay was a man of great power and privilege who played a significant role in the design of the *Titanic*. It emerged that this oligarch, immaculate in his evening dress, a man of privilege, had hopped into a lifeboat and saved himself while hundreds of others, men, women and children, perished in the freezing waters.

When news of this man's action became known it aroused outrage in the US and Britain. In his defence, and some of the class-conscious British newspapers took his part, it was said that he helped women and children into a life boat. Only when it was about to be lowered into the sea and there was room in it did he climb on board. Just the same, it looked bad that this autocrat could save himself while so many others drowned.

Nowhere was he branded a coward with such ferocity than by the all-powerful Hearst newspaper empire in the United States. He was depicted in a savage cartoon sitting safely in the lifeboat while the *Titanic* was going down and hundreds struggled for life in the icy sea.

He was given the name Brute Ismay. The Hearst newspapers declared that the white of the flag of the White Star line should be changed to a cowardly yellow.

The seeds of this malevolent hatred were said to have been sown many years before when Ismay was the shipping agent for the company in New York. He would have met Hearst socially. From all accounts they took a deep dislike to one another.

Ismay might easily have been repelled by the unscrupulous way that Hearst boosted the circulation of his newspapers. They were full of sensation, of gossip presented as facts, of shameless exaggeration. The Hearst newspapers became known as the Yellow Press.

Hearst for his part may have seen Ismay as exuding the languid self-assurance of the privileged Briton. He might have found Ismay supercilious, looking down his nose at him as a vulgar, pushy American.

At that time Hearst wanted Ismay to give interviews. Ismay refused. He was all too well aware that Hearst and his newspapers wanted stories of shipboard scandal, insobriety, violence and, ideally, murder.

Hearst, an intensely vindictive man, never forgot the rebuff. After the *Titanic* disaster his newspapers were tireless in lambasting Ismay week after week. Some of the British and international press followed suit. It served to make

Bruce Ismay one of the most despised men on the face of the earth. He resigned from the White Star Line.

Until he died in 1937, Ismay spent a long time in retreat in a modest dwelling in Connemara. It was a place of isolation and refuge for a man who had been publicly vilified internationally.

Hearst, despite his power and influence, could not prevent himself being portrayed as a heartless, malevolent bully. It was accepted that he was the inspiration for the famous film *Citizen Kane* in 1941 in which Orson Welles played the character of the ruthless tycoon.

Hearst tried to limit the distribution of the film and did all he could to harm Welles's subsequent career in movies. His resentment corroded the remaining years of his life. He died in 1951. Part of his legacy lies in the now-clichéd quip: "Don't tell my mother I'm working for Hearst newspapers. She thinks I'm playing the piano in a whorehouse."

34

CROSSING THE BAR

A place of hazard and hope

For seafarers, crossing the bar can be a very significant event. A sandbar or a barrier of rock sometimes lurks beneath the waves at the mouths of estuaries, sea inlets and bays. Vessels entering or leaving have to navigate with care as they cross the bar at its deepest place. The tides and the winds have to be taken into account to ensure a safe passage. Sometimes it's safer to have a local pilot on board.

Crossing the bar on the way into port is usually the final hurdle for a ship at the end of the voyage. And if it's a home port where the seafarers have their homes and families then getting through the gap in the sand or rock is a cause of satisfaction and elation.

Equally, crossing the bar on the way to begin a voyage means leaving relatively calm waters and heading out to the open sea. If it's stormy out there, then going out over the gap can mean saying goodbye to the sanctuary of a safe haven and being buffeted about in heavy seas.

One of the most significant bars on the Irish coastline is that which runs across the entrance to Carlingford Lough. This is a navigational challenge to ships coming and going from the ports of Greenore and Warrenpoint and, in former days, the port of Newry.

Once inside the Lough vessels are sheltered by the Mourne Mountains to the north and the Cooley range to the south and southeast. On the other hand, when ships cross the bar outward bound they find themselves in the Irish Sea, which at times can be a very rough and uncomfortable place to sail.

It was just out beyond this particular bar that a terrible tragedy took place on a stormy night in November 1916. Two ships collided with the loss of 97 lives. The *Connemara*, carrying 51 passengers from Greenore to Holyhead, had just passed the Haulbowline lighthouse that marks the bar when it met the *Retriever*, a collier inbound to Newry from Garston. Gale force winds hampered safe passage in the narrow channel just outside the bar. The *Retriever* smashed into the hull of the *Connemara*, which sank almost immediately. The collier itself was badly damaged and sank within twenty minutes. There was only one survivor, James Boyle from Warrenpoint.

The story of this marine tragedy was first told to me many years ago by a good neighbour and local historian, Jim Bruen of Omeath. Jim came from a family with a long tradition of seafaring. Nobody better than he understood the significance of the bar at the entrance to Carlingford Lough, or indeed any bar over which seafarers have to carefully navigate.

His favourite poem was, in fact, "Crossing the Bar" by Alfred Tennyson. The poet, who had a deep association with the sea, used the analogy of crossing the bar as marking the passage from life to death. In the poem, written not long before his death, Tennyson imagined himself crossing this fateful bar with fortitude and hope, unafraid to meet his Maker, whom he referred to as his Pilot.

In fact, when Jim himself died some years ago the poem was read out to a packed congregation at his funeral mass in Omeath.

This poem has a special resonance for seafarers.

Sunset and evening star
And one clear call for me!
And may there be no moaning of the bar
When I put out to sea.

Twilight and evening bell
And after that the dark
And may there be no sadness of farewell
When I embark

For tho' from out our bourne of Time and Peace
The flood may bear me far
I hope to see my Pilot face to face
When I have crossed the bar.

35

OUR CAPTAIN TOOK SALOMÉ FOR A TWIRL

A well-remembered master

Every mariner can tell stories about Captains. They are such a dominant presence in seafaring. They have many responsibilities. The Captain's personality and moods set the tone for the ship, for better or for worse.

Of the Captains I sailed under there is one particular man I remember with affection. He was a small, squat man with broad shoulders. He had a shiny bald head. His wide elastic mouth smiled easily and opened often in laughter.

His name was Leonard Bunn and he was the Captain of our deck-passenger ship the *Aronda*. We plied between Karachi on the upper edge of the Arabian Sea and Chittagon on the top of the Bay of Bengal, on the other side of the Indian sub-continent.

Lennie, as we called him, carried his responsibilities calmly. He was a good judge of character. He knew how to get the best out of people, to handle those under his command. He would say things like, "I know you'll deal with that with your usual efficiency," or "You've done a good job, thank you very much."

His policy was to let people get on with their jobs, to show them trust. Words of praise and a smile were second nature to him. He spoke some Hindi and some Urdu, and often stopped to speak with members of the crew. Our ship was a happy one.

When we were in Karachi, the agents, Mackinnon and Mackenzie, sometimes took parties of valued shippers and influential dignitaries on board for a gala night. The promenade deck was festooned with lights. A Goan band played.

Captain Bunn used to ask some of us to help act as hosts, chatting to guests, making sure their glasses were filled and taking some of the women out to dance. But when the party was over and the guests had stumbled down the gangway, he would say, "Now that we've got rid of that shower, let's have a drink," and invite us up to his cabin.

He loved a sing-song and always came forward to sing his favourite, "It's a sin to tell a lie," in a baritone voice.

There was a memorable incident in Karachi. Some of us had gone to dinner in one of the big hotels there and spotted him sitting at table with some people from the agents. He saw us and came over. He grinned. "I'm stuck with this crowd but at least there's some kind of floor show."

Sometime afterwards there was a roll of drums from the four-piece band. Then it began to play Arabic-sounding music. A girl in flimsy veils glided on to the dance floor.

She slid about sinuously, her legs and arms moving about suggestively. Then she paused and looked about the dinner tables, seeking someone on whom to demonstrate her seductive ritual. This was to be for the amusement of all the diners except for the male victim of her choice. Apparently, she usually singled out some middle-aged or even elderly man.

Lennie's bald head must have caught her attention. She swayed over to him. Without actually touching him she weaved her hands and arms around his face. There was an uneasy titter from the diners.

But she had picked on the wrong man. Lennie sprang to his feet, grabbed her round the bare waist and began to waltz her round the dance floor.

The diners were convulsed with laughter. The band switched to "The Blue Danube" waltz. We stood up at our table and applauded loudly. Eventually, Lennie gave her a peck on the cheek and let her go. He took a bow to a huge cheer.

Later, as we were leaving, a stout Pakistani businessman asked us, "Who is that jolly fellow who is waltzing that girl around the floor?"

"That's our Captain," we answered proudly.

36

WHEN THE RADAR STARTED ACTING UP

"I'll get you, you hoor you."

Radar, that marvellous navigational aid and safety system, comes into its own on dark nights at sea. The screen, with its revolving cursor, shows up the coastline, rocky islands, nearby vessels and other potential hazards.

Today's sophisticated radar sets rarely break down. However, before the era of transistors and microchips, radar sets had an array of valves, capacitors and resistors, some of which could fail. They were part of the complicated innards of the large transmission and receiver unit. This was usually housed in a metal hut above the bridge-deck of those ships whose owners could afford to install what was then a very expensive system.

One of the most common faults was the radar going off tune. The echoes of land and other ships would be replaced by aggravating, swirling lines of orange dots. Up in the radar hut, the Radio Officer would find that the needle of the tuning dial was swinging this way and that instead of being steadily upright at 90 degrees. By twiddling various knobs, he would try to coax the needle back to its proper position, thus restoring the picture on the viewing unit below on the bridge.

I first saw this vital little indicator when studying for the Radio Officer's Certificate (Second Class) in the College of Science and Technology, in Kevin Street in Dublin

Our instructor, Mr Blennerhassett, emphasised to us: "Radar is an expensive and delicate piece of equipment. It has to be treated with immense care."

The next time I saw a tuning dial on a radar was on my first ship. We carried the generally reliable Marconi Mark IV radar. However, at around midnight, as we were traversing the reef-hazardous passage between the African mainland and the islands of Zanzibar and Pemba, the radar went off tune. The Captain, who was given to fretting at the best of times, sent down for the Chief Radio Officer.

The Chief came staggering up. He was furious at being disturbed while drinking in the First Class lounge and trying to make advances to a well-seasoned lady passenger.

When we climbed up to the radar hut and removed the front cover on the big unit we could see straight away the needle of the tuning dial swaying back and forward. The Chief, with his nail-bitten fingers, began to twist and turn some of the associated tuning knobs. But the needle had a will of its own. To his fury, it didn't respond.

I soon became aware that the Chief knew almost as little about the radar as I did myself. He effed and blinded. In the hothouse of the radar hut and the heavy equatorial heat the sweaty, gin-smelling odour from his bloated pink body was overpowering. "That old bollix will blame me," he shouted, referring to the Captain, whom he hated.

All his efforts to retune came to nothing. His rage got the better of him. He sat down on the steel doorstep, braced himself by holding on to the sides of the hut. "I'll get you, you hoor you," he shouted and smashed his heels against the unit. There was a tremendous bang. The whole unit shuddered. Then, lo and behold, we saw the tuning needle quiver and return to its steady, upright position. Perhaps one of the many finely-balanced components responded to the jolt.

We scampered down to the bridge. When the Chief looked into the viewing unit he could see the coastline of Zanzibar.

The Captain approached in the semi-darkness. "Don't tell me you've fixed it, Sparks?" he said sarcastically.

"Oh, it was a complicated fault, sir, but I think I've managed to put it right," replied the Chief, with the air of someone whose knowledge and expertise had passed a severe test.

37

INVENTING THE NEWS
ON THE HIGH SEAS

Aristocratic lady's rear end savaged by camel

Who concocts spurious items of news? Tatty tabloid newspapers in France, Italy and Britain do so regularly. So do national security services. They indulge in the dissemination of false information under the guise of "protecting the interests of the state". However, news can be manufactured purely for innocuous reasons.

I myself was once involved in an episode of news creativity of the more innocent kind. The reason lay in incompetence rather than any desire to fool people. I was Radio Officer on a cargo-passenger ship of the Royal Mail Line, the *Drina*, bound for Rio de Janiero from London. At that time the British Post Office broadcast a world-wide news service for British ships at sea from Portishead Radio, located in the southwest of England.

This was long before the era of satellite TV and transistor radio. The news from Portishead was broadcast in Morse Code. The Radio Officer would take it down, have it typed up and post it on the notice board for to the news-starved passengers.

This service was provided because it was felt that no matter where a ship might be, in the South Seas or the Bight of Benin or traversing the Panama canal, British passengers would feel deprived if they couldn't hear about the latest visit of the Queen to a former colony or the ponderous pronouncements of the Chancellor of the Exchequer or the state of the wicket at Lords.

There was one problem about this news service on the *Drina*. My capability at receiving Morse was limited. I could manage twenty words a minute provided it did not go on too long. Unfortunately, the news came rippling in in an endless stream of dots and dashes for a full twenty minutes. It was sent by automatic machine. It started off at a reasonable speed, but after ten minutes the fellow in charge, obviously thirsting for a pint of good old English ale, turned up the speed. Then the Morse was zipping through the ether at 25 and eventually 28 words a minute.

Every evening in the radio room I underwent this ordeal, sitting with earphones jammed on head, scribbling furiously. The first twenty news items I managed to get down. However, after that I was liable to lose the thread, to miss words, even whole sentences.

The Master's Clerk, a decent English fellow, whose job it was to type out my scribbles and then run them off on an inky Roneo machine, used to arrive in the radio room at around 9.00 p.m. each evening, enveloped in gin fumes. He soon became aware of my limitations.

"Not to worry, old chap. Copy down the first half and we'll make up the rest."

"Make it up?"

"Oh yes. Harmless stuff. Rail crashes in India, ferry boat sinkings in the Phillipines, buses going over precipices in Afghanistan. Things like that."

That was it. We were careful not to invent any items related to South America; some of our twelve passengers might know too much about the location. However, we were both familiar with the Indian sub-continent, so it was not unexpected that the Hyderabad express would go off the rails somewhere. The driver was last seen running away from the scene of the accident, making off towards some mountainous region nearby

Riverine disasters were another source of interest. A ferry boat on the Karnaphuli river near Chittagong took fire; the Captain managed to beach the vessel and there was no loss of life. However, police had arrested the Purser since it appeared that the vessel was carrying more than twice the number of passengers for which it was licensed.

It was a source of some amusement to wander about the passenger deck after breakfast and to see some of the passengers scrutinising the "News Bulletin" pinned to the notice boards.

When we fabricated a story about an Italian passenger liner going on the rocks off the coast of Somaliland, I heard a grizzled coffee farmer say, "Treacherous coast that, I know it well. Bet it seems a typical Italian lash-up."

The Master's Clerk and I were emboldened to become more fanciful. One evening we included an item of social news.

"Lady Claire Booth-Chippenham, a distant relative of the Duke of Gloucester, was severely bitten by a camel while viewing the pyramids of Egypt."

Next morning I was astonished to hear a stout, snobbish English lady say to several others gathered round the notice board, "Oh dear, poor Lady Claire. I met her once at a garden party. It doesn't say exactly where she was bitten. Not on her face, I hope. She has beautiful features."

As a result of this special interest we decided to continue this make-believe. The following morning the item on the notice board read:

"Doctors in Cairo have treated the seriously bitten posterior of Lady Claire Booth-Chippenham, who was savaged by a camel while viewing the Pyramids. A bulletin on her condition will be issued by the hospital later. A message of concern from the Duke of Gloucester has been conveyed to her."

This caused a stir among the passengers. Some did not take kindly to the notion of swarthy Egyptian male doctors viewing or even pressing the shapely, aristocratic buttocks of Lady Claire under the guise of medical treatment.

However the most significant outcome was some bad feeling between two of the passengers. Apparently the snobbish lady irked some of them with her loud, assertive claims to know Lady Claire. One was a thin, acerbic minor British diplomat on his way to take up his role as Assistant Third Secretary in the consulate in Rio de Janeiro.

He had with him a copy of *Burke's Peerage*, that genealogical guide to Britain's gentry that ambitious diplomats of that era regarded as essential. This fellow pored over the filigree of dukes, lords, barons and their family trees, but nowhere could he find a relationship between the Duke of Gloucester and someone called Lady Claire Booth-Chippenham. In fact, nobody of that family name appeared anywhere in this revered tome.

That evening at dinner this undiplomatic fellow told the lady and the assembled passengers of his fruitless search. She bridled. Sharp words were exchanged between them. Our Captain, who presided at the table, assumed the role of peacemaker. He offered a tactful explanation: "It could well be that the name got garbled in transmission in Morse code."

He appeared unexpectedly in the radio room later, where the Master's Clerk and I were in the act of merrily juggling our imaginations to create news for next day's notice board.

He eyed both of us keenly as he related what had transpired at the dinner table. He may have got a whiff of gin. Then he said, with some authority: "Look, let's have no more about this Lady Claire person and her arse being bitten by a camel. And from now on don't put anything in the News Bulletin that we can't stand over."

He gave a faint grin before departing. We could never be sure if he suspected what had been going on. He never mentioned the subject again.

That was the end of our foray into news invention. It didn't matter very much because by that time we were off the coast of Brazil and the passengers' minds were on disembarking on our arrival in Rio.

38

FORGOTTEN LANGUAGE OF THE AIRWAVES

Dots and dashes once rippled over the airwaves

In some public place, on a bus or a train, in a café or restaurant, the beeping sounds ring out from sombody's mobile phone. Di di di – dah dah – di di di. These short and long rhythmic pulses indicate that a message awaits the mobile owner.

Probably few of the mobile users or those in the vicinity realise that the sounds are actually in Morse Code. They form the initials of the Short Messaging Service – S-M-S – three dots, two dashes, three dots. This is one of the very rare occasions when Morse is still used.

That sound has great resonance for anyone who used Morse as the means of communication, most especially at sea. More than that, the two dashes of the "M" are only one dash short of making it into an "O" which would turn it into S-**O**-S, the international distress signal.

Radio men aboard ship sat up when they heard this call on their receivers. They fine-tuned the signal, turned up the volume, clamped their earphones on their heads and immediately notified the Captain. Sometimes, if the stricken vessel was within sailing distance, it meant changing course and racing towards it, while Morse messages flew back and forth.

Morse transmitters and receivers became part of safety at sea soon after the Italian inventor Marconi showed that signals could be sent and received across wave and headland at the start of the last century. Passenger ships began to install radio equipment and the men to operate it.

One of the first and certainly most dramatic episodes of the use of Morse at sea was in 1912 when the Titanic sent out pitiful signals for help. "We have struck an ice berg," said one of them. The wireless operators on the *Titanic* stuck to their posts in the radio room to the very last; they were lost with the ship.

By the time of the outbreak of war in 1939, *all* deep-sea ships had wireless equipment and Radio Officers. Their role was highlighted by the hostilities at sea. Radio men tapped out chilling, frantic or doleful messages on their Morse keys, telling of attack by submarines, airplanes and warships of various kinds.

They were expected to keep sending out the SOS, giving the position of the ship to possible rescuers, until they had no option but to abandon the radio room and jump over the side. Sometimes the attackers aimed the first gunfire at the radio room to try to quieten such calls for help.

Many Irishmen went to sea as Radio Officers. Most of them joined the company set up by Marconi because, in this country, there was exceptional interest in him and his experiments. His mother was one of the Jamesons of whiskey fame who lived in Montrose House, still standing on the grounds of RTÉ in Dublin. The "Father of Radio", as he was called, conducted many of his transatlantic experiments in wireless communication from stations along the Irish coastline, including a major installation at Clifden.

For well over 100 years the dots and dashes of Morse sounded on the airwaves. However, greatly improved voice radio gradually took over. Morse was still in use for long-distance messages until relatively recently. Then, highly sophisticated satellite telephone systems were introduced. As their cost to marine users became more affordable, it spelt the end of Morse as a general means of marine communication.

The last Morse signals from Valentia Radio Station in Kerry were sent out at midnight on Sunday, 31 January 1999, to end the station's Morse service for shipping. Now, only an occasional echo of this once-widespread language of the airwaves is heard from somebody's mobile phone.

39

ONCE A CAPTAIN

From a sleek cargo liner to a rusty dredger

When a ship is wrecked the Captain has to take responsibility. He may lose his Master's Certificate or have it suspended. Most likely, he'll get the sack from the shipping company.

The blot on his record may haunt his career. If he wants to stay at sea, doing the only job he knows, he has to take whatever he can find, in whatever part of the world it may be.

I came across one such person quite a few years ago. At Manora, the port of Karachi, under the searing summer heat and the scorching wind that came out of the Sind desert, a rusty old dredger creaked and squealed hour after hour. The dripping chain of heavy iron buckets groaned and grated as they moved upwards endlessly.

Our deck-passenger ship was tied up nearby. We were undergoing our annual overhaul. We plied between Karachi and the port of Chittagong, on the other side of the Indian sub-continent, calling at Colombo on the way there and back.

The prolonged stay in Karachi was not pleasant. We had no air conditioning. The sand from the nearby desert often created a burning brown haze. The grains got into our eyelids and between our teeth and into our ears.

What made the whole experience worse was that for much of the daylight hours we were within sight and sound of the endless whining and rasping of that battered old dredger. We couldn't keep out the sound any more than we could keep the sand out of our clothes.

One night in the bar of a seedy hotel in Karachi, a few of us found ourselves in the company of a fat, sweating Englishman of advanced middle age. His face was beetroot red, partly from the effects of sun and glare and, we reckoned, also something to do with the amount of alcohol he consumed. But he was a jolly fellow who laughed easily.

It turned out that he was the Captain of the dredger. He was there every evening in the bar. I suppose he welcomed the company of other Europeans, as he spent all day trying to communicate with his Pakistani crew in a mixture of Hindustani, Urdu and English. As a result, when he was fairly well on, he relapsed into this odd lingual mixture.

One night he told us the stories of his misfortunes. He did so as if they were funny adventures, sometimes bursting into laughter.

He had once been Captain of a modern cargo liner on her maiden voyage from London to the Far East. Unfortunately. at 2.00 in the morning, as that pristine vessel approached Colombo, the Second Mate took ill. To make matters worse, the radar packed in.

The Captain was called. He was out on the wing of the bridge focusing his binoculars on nearby coastal lights when there was a great crunching sound as the ship piled on to rocks not too far from the entrance to the port.

There was no loss of life or injury, but the ship was a write off. He was sacked. He eventually got a job as Captain of a little steamer plying the coasts of Burma and Malaysia. That lasted several years until the steamer collided with another ship in a narrow strait. He burst into laughter as he said, "I was sacked – again." So he had fetched up on the dirty old dredger.

Some weeks afterwards, as we approached Colombo, the Third Mate and I stood on the wing of the bridge, training the binoculars on the wreck that had blighted that Captain's career. We could see its masts sticking up at an angle; most of its rusting superstructure was above water. It was a sad sight.

But the Third Mate smiled and said, "I sincerely hope we'll be able to handle our own misfortunes with the same spirit as that man."

40

DICTATORSHIP AND THE PRICE OF A PINT

Three Cheers for Democracy

Whenever I hear someone say that they're not going to vote, or they give out about the flaws in our democratic system, I'm reminded of a voyage I made many years ago. I was the Radio Officer on a ship which went to South America to load beef for the British market.

Our first loading port was Buenos Aires, capital of the Argentine. On our arrival there the shipping agent came on board. Like many Argentinians, he was a man of Italian background. He had an important warning to impart to us all.

"We got the military rule here in Argentina. In a bar or some kind of dive, don't get into a fight OK? Otherwise police come, everybody gets arrested. Who knows what happens", he shrugged his shoulders to indicate menace.

With these warnings in our ears we strolled about the streets of this great city, a vibrant place full of life and energy, resounding with the rhythm of the tango. But we were careful. We saw the bullet marks on the front of the Casa

Rosada, the presidential palace that had been stormed by the army in its successful coup.

We then set off for Brazil, passing almost within sight of Uruguay, which also was under military rule at the time. We arrived at Porto Alegre, in the southern part of Brazil. We had hardly tied up alongside when a blond man, representing the agents, came on board. Like many in that part of Brazil, he was German. Almost the very first words he uttered were a warning.

"We have now in control the colonels. A putsch, you understand. The president is ousted. Military rule. Better for nobody to get into trouble in bars and ... other places."

So here we were, going about with some caution in one of the largest and most populous countries in the world, a country of endless diversity, of great wealth and poverty, of colour, of the smell of coffee and exotic tobacco, of the sound of the samba and Brazilian-accented Portuguese.

We eventually set sail for Europe. Brazil is so vast that it took us five days to clear the coast of this country where the military ruled. After another five days we were abreast of Africa. In the radio room I began hearing signals of the marine radio stations in the Canary Islands. They and the Spanish mainland were then under the repressive dictatorship of General Franco. At much the same time the stations in Madeira and in Lisbon could be heard. At that time Portugal had been decades under the dictatorship of one Dr Salazar. The jails of the Iberian peninsula were full of political detainees.

At long last, after three weeks sailing in the shadow of military rulers and dictators of one kind or another, our ship reached the Bay of Biscay. That evening I switched the main transmission aerial into the receiver. With earphones on head I managed to tune in and amplify the sound of Radio Éireann on the medium wave.

I heard a news report. An item was introduced about a protest at the price of the pint of stout. There was a by-election campaign in one of the Dublin constituencies. Apparently a government minister – it may have been the Minister for Finance – had entered some pub in Inchicore to canvass for votes. Instead, some irate drinker poured a glass of stout over him, as a way of protesting at the price.

According to the report, the minister took this extreme gesture with a certain amount of grace and moved on. The perpetrator wasn't even cautioned let alone arrested.

While I would never condone such loutish behaviour, at the same time I found myself smiling and saying aloud, "Three cheers for democracy."

41

GETTING THE BETTER OF THE PROHIBITION POLICE

"Who ever heard of gin prunes!"

As our passenger ship tied up alongside Alexandra pier in Bombay and the gangways went clattering down, the team of Prohibion Policemen came forward in their smart dark purple uniforms.

The job of these zealous fellows was to see to it that no alcohol of any kind was taken on to the soil of the State of Bombay. The strict ban on the sale and consumption of alcohol was being rigorously enforced. As soon as they came on board they sealed the bar.

Our ship, of course, was well-stocked with a wide range of spirits and beers. The Captain and officers were European, mostly British. Many drank heavily. It was a consolation for having to endure the heat and humidity that enclosed one like a hot wet blanket. Alcohol didn't cure heat rash or dhobi itch or homesickness or insect bites but it made them easier to put up with.

Prohibition was a sore trial for many. Among those who tried hardest to get the better of it were the Irish Radio Officers on Eastern Service, attached to the Bombay office of the Marconi Company. We served on ships of the Mogul line and the British India company in the 1950s.

My boss, the Chief Radio Officer, took some risks. Our cabins were routinely searched after we docked. They sometimes pulled out the drawers and shone torches along the dark spaces behind.

However, they were in awe of the radio room. It had an air of importance about it, with its impressive array of transmitters, receivers, automatic alarm and other equipment. Their search was no more than a respectful casting of eyes around before departing.

Thankfully, they were unaware that behind the polished grey metal covers of the transmitters, bottles of gin, whisky, vodka and brandy had been laid along the tops of the valves – delicate devices that the technical manuals stressed were to be treated with the utmost care.

One of the most memorable episodes of outwitting prohibition arose when a dinner party was planned in one of the big hotels. The challenge was to have alcohol of some kind to enliven the evening. But it would be too risky to try to carry bottles down the gangway. The police were always around.

Then one of the great characters of the Indian Coast, Billy Bradshaw, a fine and decent man from Tipperary town, came up with a clever solution. He ordered a large bag of stoned prunes in one of the markets and had it hauled on board. His ship was heading up to the Red Sea to Jeddah.

The prunes were laid out on several trays and taken to the very top deck of the ship. They lay there in the sizzling sun day after day. They shrank until they looked like small, wizened black stones.

The next stage was to put them into large jars. Then gin was poured in on top of them. By the time the ship arrived back in Bombay the prunes had absorbed the gin and regained their original size and look.

On the night of the party the gin prunes were taken ashore in a transparent sack. The Prohibition Police merely glanced at them, assumed they were a consignment of ordinary prunes.

We all assembled at a table for twenty, guests, friends, girl friends. We asked for four or five plates and for toothpicks. When these were laid on the table the prunes were poured out. They lay there, soggy with gin, their black skins glistening under the table lights.

Soon, arms stretched out to spear a gin prune with a toothpick and mouths opened wide to take it in.

By the end of the night our table was in uproar. When we eventually started to leave one of our male guests lost his footing and tumbled down some steps. An Indian friend of ours shook his head and said: "No party is complete unless some fellow down the stairs is falling. Just the same it's better than getting run over by a speeding taxi."

42

A LINE THAT SAVED LIVES

The Plimsoll Line

In the nineteenth century the term "coffin ship" came into usage in the English-speaking world. Especially in Ireland it referred to those unseaworthy and overloaded ships carrying Irish emigrants fleeing from the Great Famine of 1845–1848. Several went down in mid-ocean with loss of all lives on board.

In Britain the term "coffin ship" was applied to those decrepit vessels that had been heavily insured by their unscrupulous owners. They were actually worth more if they sank than if they remained afloat.

Such ships were often overloaded with cargo. This was done in the interest of profit, even if it put the lives of the crew at serious risk.

Of course, overloading vessels was nothing new. It was recorded in the Kingdom of Crete that measures to counter this malpractice were introduced in the year 2500 BC.

In the Middle Ages the Venetian republic, the city of Genoa and the Hanseatic League all required ships to load to a safe level. In Venice, the safe load line was indicated by a cross marked on the side of the vessel, while in Genoa it was three horizontal lines.

In the nineteenth century, Britain had become the leading international trading country. There were powerful shipping companies and hundreds of ships of all kinds. Unfortunately, overloading was commonplace. Many ships went down because of it.

It was in the 1860s that a British Member of Parliament, Samuel Plimsoll, began a campaign for the establishment of a safe load line for ships. An impressive man with a domed forehead and big moustache and beard, this radical politician had once suffered destitution. He had come to know the Victorian underworld of the downtrodden. He developed an immense sympathy for the plight of badly-paid sailors whose lives were put at risk by greedy owners.

In 1872 he published a book called *Our Seamen.* It called for greater safety measures to protect seafarers from exploitation and unnecessary danger. The book caused a stir. Plimsoll's efforts resulted in the government introducing a bill in 1875.

However, it was vigorously opposed by a number of MPs who came from ship-owning families or had close associations with owners. As a result, the Prime Minister, Benjamin Disraeli, dropped the bill.

Plimsoll was outraged. During an angry debate he called his opponents "villains". Then, in an unusual breach of parliamentary behaviour, he shook his fist in the Speaker's face.

For this he was excluded from the House of Commons for some time. Eventually, he had to apologise. But the dramatic row attracted such public attention that the government was eventually forced to pass a bill. This required every individual ship to carry a mark that indicated the safe limit to which it could be loaded. Equally important, stringent powers of inspection were given to the British Board of Trade to ensure that this was carried out.

The safe load line indicator became known as the Plimsoll Line. The original mark was the circle with the horizontal line through it. Additional marks have been added. There is an indicator that looks like a simple stylised drawing of an upright tree with some horizontal branches; these denote the slightly different loading levels for fresh water or for salt water, for tropic seas or for colder waters.

Of course, there were concerns for marine safety in other seafaring countries, and there were parallel methods of indicating and enforcing safe loading lines. It was not until 1930 that there was an international agreement for universal application of load line regulations.

Samuel Plimsoll is remembered for his care for seafarers and for the Plimsoll Line. A monument to his memory stands on the Victoria Embankment in London, overlooking that stretch of the River Thames where ships were once loaded and sometimes overloaded many years before.

43

SAD END TO VOYAGE OF
EUSTACE THE WARTHOG

"I looked after him as if he was
he best friend I ever had."

I heard an unusual story about a warthog, a ferocious-looking member of the pig family. The fellow who told me was a Cadet on a cargo ship that transported the animal from Africa to Liverpool, destined for a zoo in Northern England.

"It was loaded on board in a big wooden cage in the port of Luanda, in Angola. Everyone on board came out to see this wild creature."

A man from the zoo, who had bought the warthog locally, was on hand to look after this beast. He supervised the placing of the cage on a selected part of the deck, where an awning was erected to protect the animal from the sun and to let in fresh air and light. Bales of fodder were loaded on board – grasses, roots, berries – as well as straw to cover the floor of the cage.

Then, on the evening before sailing, the custodian of the warthog went on the tear in a seedy part of the city. He was last seen in the company of a buxom local woman. He never appeared on the morning of sailing.

The Captain was furious. "We can't wait for him. We'll go without him. We'll look after the warthog ourselves."

When they set sail he called the Cadet. "You're in charge of the warthog. You must look after it as if it was the dearest friend you ever had."

The Cadet was at first uneasy about the responsibility placed on him. He was cautious. He stood carefully outside the cage. He noticed the upward-curved tusks and the razor sharp lower set. On the head were four wart-like lumps that gave the creature its name.

After a while both boy and beast began to relax in one another's company. The warthog knew that the Cadet was the source of its food, and would come and place its snout against the wooden posts of the cage at mealtime. After awhile the Cadet leaned in and tickled its head.

There was no question that he would enter the cage. He used a long-handled brush to sweep out the floor and to lay a covering of fresh straw.

He christened it Eustace because it reminded him of an uncle of that name who had very prominent teeth. All the crew came to see it.

The Captain came down every day to watch Eustace. On several occasions he sent radio messages to the zoo, reporting on the animal's condition.

Everyone got concerned when the ship passed the Canary Islands and headed towards the Bay of Biscay. There the temperature dropped and the sea became rough. A heater was set up outside the cage and Eustace huddled nearby. He made a sort of burrow for himself out of straw and lay low.

Cadet and Captain were relieved when the ship docked in Liverpool. Two men from the zoo – probably Chester zoo – came on board and declared Eustace to be in fine fettle. They thanked the Captain. The Cadet was taken aback to overhear the Captain saying, "I looked after him personally as if he was the best friend I ever had."

The whole crew came out to watch the cage being swung over the side by one of the ship's derricks. Someone shouted, "Goodbye Eustace, old chap."

Then disaster. The cage hit the railings with a loud bang. Two of the wooden staves were knocked out. Eustace, in a state of terror, escaped, running along the deck. Then he fell down a companion way and broke his leg. He lay there squealing. The men from the zoo had no option but to put him down with a humane killer.

Everyone felt sad watching the carcass of the warthog in a sling being swung over the side to the dock below.

The Cadet heard someone say, "God knows Eustace was as ugly as sin, but he wasn't a bad creature just the same."

44

"WOMEN AND CHILDREN FIRST"

Soldiers stood to attention as ship went under

"Women and children first." This graphic phrase evokes pictures of passenger ships listing dangerously. The lifeboats are swung out, ready to be boarded. Then, in the best traditions of seafaring, women and children are given priority over men, especially over members of the crew.

In many cases, where some lifeboats are damaged or it is impossible to swing all of them out from steeply slanting decks, staying behind can mean facing possible death. There simply isn't room for all.

For some of those men clinging to railings on the stricken vessel, wondering when it will go under, it must take a great deal of self-control to stem the panic of desperation that urges them to save their own lives by jumping on board an overcrowded lifeboat.

Others, especially naval and military personnel, may have been trained and mentally pre-conditioned on how to act on such hazardous occasions. They know what their duties are, what they have to do. They are prepared to take the risk of drowning with a certain hardiness of spirit.

In British seafaring lore, the orderly abandonment of a sinking ship, with the safety of women and children being given the utmost importance, was most uniquely epitomised by events on the troopship *Birkenhead*. This happened in February 1852 as the ship was on her way from Cape Town to Algoa Bay, carrying some 640 people, mostly soldiers of the 73rd Regiment of Foot, but also the wives and children of officers.

At 2.00 in the morning, on a calm, clear night, she struck an uncharted rock at a place called Danger Point. Water rushed in the large hole, flooding the for'ard part of the ship. Over 100 soldiers were drowned in their berths. The remainder were mustered on deck. They stood to attention on the slanting deck in their red uniforms as the crew tried to get the women and children into whatever lifeboats could be launched.

The soldiers did not move even when the ship broke up, barely twenty minutes after impaling itself on the rock. At the end some managed to swim to the shore which was about two miles away, hanging on to pieces of wreckage to stay afloat. But many were drowned, died of exposure or taken by sharks.

In a subsequent enquiry, the orderliness, discipline and valour of the soldiers was so emphasised that the phrase, Birkenhead Drill, was coined. It stood for courageous behaviour in hopeless circumstances.

The term got wider prominence when that Poet Laureate of the British Empire, Rudyard Kipling, used it in a poem praising the virtues of the men of the British army and navy.

However, this national pride sometimes led British seafarers to look down on races they considered less courageous and honourable than themselves. They sometimes took delight in recounting stories about some Greek or Italian marine disaster. The captain, instead of following in the stiff-upper lip tradition of being last to leave the sinking vessel, was in fact among the very first to abandon ship. Or the crew scrambled into the lifeboats, leaving the hapless passengers to fend for themselves.

And indeed there was a less heroic side to the soldiers on the *Birkenhead*. They were part of a military force being sent to subjugate a South African tribe that did not take kindly to being forced off their traditional lands by the incursions of European settlers. The Xhosa warriors, with their cow-hide shields and spears, were no match for the modern field artillery of the British army, or the rifles and disciplined firepower of the men in red uniforms.

45

DISASTROUS TANGO DANCING IN BUENOS AIRES

Like a baby elephant on the dance floor

Before the invention of radio and the first gramophone recordings well over 100 years ago, sailors played a role, however small, in popularising some forms of music and dance.

They picked up a dance or a song or a rhythm in a foreign port and carried it back home. This happened with that exotic Argentinian dance, the tango.

At the end of the nineteenth century it flourished in the smoky, noisy dancehalls and seedy dives in the great port cities of Buenos Aires and Montevideo.

It radiated a steamy sensuality. The tango is a mixture of European and African rhythms. The dance mesmerised seafarers who witnessed the writhing, sinuous movement of a couple dancing body-to-body to a strange thumping tempo.

Soon, various versions of the tango were being heard along the waterfronts in Genoa, Marseilles, Rotterdam and Hamburg. German sailors introduced the bandoneon, a kind of concertina, to Buenos Aires and it joined the violin, piano and flute in the tango orchestra.

Then, at the start of the twentieth century the recording industry began to emerge. In the late twenties and early thirties the tango was elevated from its sleazy beginnings and gained tremendous popularity all over the Spanish-speaking world, as well as in Europe and the US.

Many years later I had an uneasy encounter with the tango. Our cargo ship, the *Drina* of the Royal Mail Line, was berthed alongside the waterfront of Buenos Aires. Tango bars and dance halls were just across the road.

One night I went ashore with Dougie, the Second Mate, to watch the spectacle in a big smoky place. Angular men with greased black hair in black suits danced with voluptuous women in body-hugging dresses and split skirts. A lot of leg and thigh was on display during the sensuous performances.

In all the clamour of music and loud talk a girl came round to the tables selling tickets. I bought one, thinking it was for a raffle for a hamper of some sort.

Then the music stopped and a glamorous lady dancer in a red low-cut dress called for silence. She held up a ticket and called out a number.

Dougie looked at my raffle ticket: "Hey you've won the prize."

"What prize?"

"To get up and dance the tango with that beauty."

I wanted to slink away. But all eyes were turned in my direction. I got to my feet very reluctantly. The lady stretched out her bare arm and beckoned me to come to her.

She pulled me towards her and put my arm around her waist. She pressed her rouged face against mine and said in a low seductive tone: "Don't be afraid – I won't bite you. Come on. *Vamonos* – let's go."

The band struck up, to a great cheer from the crowd. She did all the movements, pulling me along with her. I did my best but my feet seemed to slip this way and that, like Charlie Chaplin trying to keep his feet on an over-waxed ballroom floor. This was a long, long way from doing an old-time waltz in the Confraternity Hall in Thurles.

The audience began to laugh. The laughter got louder and reached a climax when I slipped and fell backwards, nearly pulling my voluptuous companion down on top of me. With that she signalled to the band and they played an end-of-dance fanfare.

I staggered back to the table. The Second Mate with his dry English humour said, "I'm sorry to have to tell you, Old Chap, but you were rather like a baby elephant out there."

Not so long ago I heard a musician at the National Concert Hall say that the tango could be as difficult to play as to dance. I think I know what he was talking about.

46

THE FEARFUL POINT
OF NO RETURN

"Would you ever take a look at that man's back."

When seafarers talk about "the point of no return" they often do so with unease. It may mean that the ship or indeed the yacht has gone so far that there can be no turning back, no matter what goes wrong.

It may be a point so far out to sea that engine break-downs, fires, injuries or illnesses may have to be coped with – without hope of immediate help.

One afternoon, quite a few years ago, on one of the cargo-passenger vessels of the Ellerman Line, *The City of Bedford*, the ship's doctor looked anxiously at a chart of the Pacific Ocean. We were in Savannah, Georgia, in the United States, to pick up both cargo and twelve passengers. From there we were to set sail for the Panama Canal and then undertake the long, six-weeks voyage to Brisbane in Australia.

The large-scale chart of the Pacific showed a vast, empty ocean, except for a few tiny dots that denoted islands. Even the land mass of the Americas on the right hand margins of the map and the bulk of Australasia away over on the left seemed insignificant compared with the immensity of the Pacific.

"That's the point of no return," said this small, middle-aged doctor from County Meath, putting his finger on a place a few days voyaging out of Panama.

Despite his great sense of humour and genial cheerfulness, our doctor was worried. He was afraid that some of our passengers might take ill during the long Pacific passage, and that his rusty and uncertain medical skills might be called upon.

Only passengers who were well off could afford the cost of the long voyage. Invariably, some would be elderly. Our decent doctor had nightmares at the prospect of trying to perform an operation in mid-ocean, such as removing an inflamed appendix.

He was afraid that if somebody died, he might be blamed for his lack of medical expertise.

He knew he should never have been a doctor. Like many of his kind, he had found a place at sea, joining the long cavalcade of unsuitable and alcoholic doctors that people the pages of seafaring reminiscences.

Our crew were Indian. Occasionally one of them came to him. His treatment was fairly basic. For any pain in the area of the head, aspirin was prescribed. Any pain in the region of the stomach called for a good dose of what was called black draught. This was a powerful purgative that scoured out the intestines and the bowels.

However, the head of the crew, the serang, had a recurrent back problem that refused to respond to any such simple remedies. He often knocked on the door of the doctor's cabin or the ship's surgery seeking relief, but without any success.

"That serang has me crucified with his back," complained our doctor cheerfully. "I don't know what to do with him."

As soon as he heard that our passengers were boarding, he went below to look them over.

Twenty minutes later he burst into my cabin, chuckling. "Would you believe it but one of the passengers is a retired US Army doctor," he said. "He has a clatter of medical qualifications after his name. If anything goes seriously wrong with any of those passengers, he can take over. I'll act as his assistant if he has to operate," he said with happy relief. He opened a bottle of whisky. With a mischievous grin, he said, "I think I'll get him to have a look at the serang's back." That night he fell into bed, joyfully drunk.

As they were sitting at the same table in the saloon, he and the US Army man struck up a friendship, exchanging yarns of medical adventures and experiences. Then, after a fitting amount of time had passed, he mentioned the serang's back problem.

"Let me have a look at it," the Army man said.

That afternoon, when the serang lay face-down on the table in the surgery, he ran his hands down the man's spine. "Got it. A disc has popped out," he said. "I've seen plenty of these in the army." Then he pressed on the disc and returned it to its proper position on the serang's spine.

After the serang had gone away, his pain and discomfort relieved, the two medics sat down and enjoyed several shots from the medicinal bottle of brandy that was usually kept in one of the cabinets in case some emergency called for it.

As it happened, we passed the point of no return in the wide Pacific without any kind of medical crisis and after a long voyage eventually reached the port of Brisbane in Queensland, Australia.

47

HE SURPRISED HIS UNFAITHFUL WIFE WITH LOVER

"If he hadn't escaped I'd have killed him."

Infidelity can be a serious matter for seafarers. Men are away at sea, sometimes for weeks, sometimes for months. The wife or partner is left at home, minding the children, minding the house. Loneliness can make them crave for the intimacies of love.

Married seafarers can find themselves in a foreign port after a long spell at sea. They can find themselves chatting in some bar to some friendly women. Temptation often presents itself, aided by the amount of drink taken.

I heard a harrowing story of infidelity and its aftermath, from a member of the crew of our ship, the ore carrier *Monksgarth*. We were sailing across the North Atlantic to load at the port of Sept Isles in Quebec. The weather was getting cold but every day I noticed this burly, bald-headed man pacing up and down the lower deck, dressed only in denim trousers and a vest.

He worked in the engine-room, greasing and oiling the machinery. His name was Joe Cowley and he came from the northeast coastal region of England. One afternoon he came up to the radio room and asked me to send a telegram to his sister to wish her a happy birthday. He stayed there while I tapped it out on Morse to Portishead radio on short wave. Then we got chatting.

He had an intimidating look about him. He had a jutting lower jaw and two hard eyes that looked out from beneath a heavy forehead. Wiry grey hair covered his chest and arms.

When I asked him if he was married, his lips tightened and he he closed his fists. Then he told me his story.

He had been married with two children. "I sent her everything, I saved up for the house, every penny."

One time when he was home from the sea he met a friend of his in the local pub. This man said, "Joe, you and I are good friends, aren't we?"

"Yes we are Jack, why?"

"It's about Mabel."

"I'll break your neck if you're wrong."

"You're away at sea and I'm here. I know what goes on. She's not playing fair by you,"

He said that normally when he was coming home on leave he would send a telegram and Mabel would meet him at the station.

"She'd say 'I'm so glad your back, Joe, I have your favourite meal ready, Joe.'"

However the next time he was coming home he sent no telegram. "I went round the back, put my case in the shed. Then I went in the back door quietly. She was nowhere to be seen. Then I heard voices from the bedroom upstairs. I ran up the stairs. He was putting on his shoes. I remember grabbing a bronze statue of he Blessed Virgin and smashing in into his face. I can tell you one thing – if he hadn't got away I'd have killed him. He pushed me onto the floor and escaped down the stairs.

The dirty, lying bitch was screaming her head off. I knocked her flat with one blow. I put my two thumbs into her neck as far as they would go. I'd have killed her only the neighbours and then the police came.

She told them I had attacked her for no reason. I told them, 'Look for a fellow with a bandage round his face.'"

Cowley was arrested and put in jail to await trial for attempted murder, assault and grievous bodily harm. On the day of the court case he said to the judge, "I want her out of my house. She did me wrong."

The judge replied, "Mr Cowley are you not aware that the house and all it's contents are in your wife's name."

"But they're mine, they're mine. I spent two years in the Antarctic on a whaling trip, a cruel unnatural life. I sent home every penny."

"Your wife is legally entitled to everything."

He was sentenced to three years in jail.

"Before I left the dock I said to the judge, 'As sure as God's above, as sure as you're sitting on that bench, as soon as I get out of jail I'll find her and I'll wring her neck.'"

The court made a barring order that he was not to go near the house when he came out of jail.

Even now, telling me his story some years later, this bear-like man's face was dark with anger and his massive fists were clenched.

"A friend told me she never lived there again. May she never be happy as long as she lives."

From then on, every time I saw him pacing the deck I thought about his terrible story and eventually wrote it down in a notebook.

48

A CYCLONE IN THE ARABIAN SEA

Too busy to be seasick

We had no idea what was in store for us. It seemed that one more uneventful voyage lay ahead. As our gangways were being hauled up at the dusty port of Karachi, the sun was blazing down out of a hot blue sky.

Many of our 1,800 passengers lined the railings, waving goodbye to their friends gathered on the quayside below. Then our 8,000 ton deck-passenger ship, the *Aronda*, headed out to sea. We soon turned south-south-east, heading for Colombo.

Only when I went to the radio room to do my two-hour watch did I become aware that stormy weather loomed. Coastal radio stations were sending out streams of urgent Morse Code. They warned those within earshot that a cyclone was churning far out in the western Arabian Sea. It was heading slowly but steadily towards the Indian subcontinent.

I went up to the bridge with this weather warning. As the Second Mate marked the cyclone centre on the chart he said: "They're rare enough in the Arabian Sea. But when they do happen they can hoover up small craft, fishing boats and dhows. They can sweep away fishing villages and low lying places." He reckoned it would be at least 36 hours before we would be affected by the oncoming storm.

Our ship participated in a system of world-wide marine weather reporting. The Second Mate immediately took the barometric pressure, assessed the wind speed and direction and the state of the sea. He calculated our position. He then translated all this information into a series of five-figure codes. He then gave them to me to send off to the international weather bureau.

It was over 24 hours later before we began to see the signs. The wind started to howl and scattered fragments of cloud raced forward from the western horizon.

It was sometime before midnight that the storm became severe. Our ship heaved slowly from side to side. The calendar on the bulkhead of the radio room swung back and forward like a slow pendulum. The pencils ran to and fro across the desk.

The airwaves were frantic with streams of hurried Morse as the Bombay marine radio station coordinated the rescue of small fishing boats by nearby ships and vessels of the Indian Navy.

We had problems trying to send our weather reports. As the ship swayed and heaved, our aerial, connected to the masts high above the deck, began to brush against the radar hut. Whenever this happened the current shorted and our transmitter tripped. Myself and the chief Radio Officer, Jimmy Wilson from Bangor, County Down, had to go up top. In the roaring gale we held on to handrails for dear life. After a struggle in the torrential rain and in semi-darkness we managed to tighten the aerial.

This was a time of great misery for our passengers. The Third Mate told us that many were wretched with sea-sickness and some were calling out in alarm.

Then the cyclone passed over the coastline of India and the winds and rain quickly died down. Evidently, it had not been too severe. Very few lives were lost. By morning the wind slackened off rapidly, the seas calmed down and the sun shone out of a blue, cloudless sky.

There was a sad postscript. A middle-aged man, apparently in a state of panic during the storm, had suffered a fatal heart attack. In the afternoon the ship went to slow speed and his body, wrapped in canvas and weighted with lead bars, was slowly lowered over the side. The passengers stood at the railings, watching this ceremony.

Jimmy Wilson said: "It's difficult for passengers. It's all right for us – we have to work away at our jobs. We haven't time to become fearful or even seasick."

49

A STORY IN PRAISE OF DRINK

"Good job he was on it that night"

The Mate on our ship was a heavy drinker. It didn't affect the way this jolly fellow from Aberdeen carried out his duties. Yet in subtle ways he emphasised the benefits of alcohol, as he saw them.

He often talked about Charles Joughin, who became famous as the last person to step off the railings of the *Titanic* just before she went under. Joughin said that he had drunk more than a bottle of spirits a short time before.

It was widely accepted that he survived the freezing waters because of the alcohol levels in his blood. And many said that his unruffled behaviour as he swam about, clung to an upturned lifeboat and was eventually among those rescued was because the alcohol had helped soothe any fears and panic he might have felt.

Our Mate said: "If it hadn't been for the drink he'd have died."

He had his own story in praise of drink. During World War II he was Third Mate on a cargo ship bound for the UK from Argentina with grain and meat.

It was a time of great danger and stress. U-boats had sunk several ships off the West African coast.

The ship was sailing alone, not part of any protected convoy. Men slept in their uniforms or heavy clothes with the strap of their life-jackets wrapped around one arm.

"Our Captain was a heavy drinker, but some busybody in Buenos Aires warned him to go on the dry for our dangerous voyage. After a few days without drink he became cranky, complained about everything. He was nervous, very jittery. We had life-boat drills that ended up with him shouting his head off at everyone, giving contradictory orders. Among ourselves we were very worried about him being in charge in a real emergency."

The tension grew as the ship neared the West African coast. It was made worse, according to our Mate, by the Captain constantly barking at the lookouts on the wings of the bridge who were scanning the seas with binoculars.

But they came safely away from the danger area and were heading past the Canaries. The stress began to lift. Only a few more days and they would see the English coast.

"Then we noticed a complete change in our Captain. He smiled and joked and spoke words of friendship and encouragement to everyone. We peeped into his cabin and saw him sitting there with a bottle of brandy on his desk and a contented smile on his face."

But at 2.00 in the morning the ship was heaved upwards by a frightening explosion. They had been struck by a torpedo.

As our Mate told it, the Captain emerged from his cabin, radiating calm. His soothing tones were heard over the PA. "All right men. No panic. Take your time. It's time to abandon ship. God bless you all. You're good men and you'll survive."

Both lifeboats were launched. Our Mate said that the Captain was the last to leave, making his way with great dignity to the railings, uniform cap on head and a canvas bag with the ship's log book under his arm.

"In the lifeboat we were full of admiration for the way he balanced himself on the railings, slid down into the sea, took hold of an oar and was hauled on board," he said.

They were rescued the next day by a British destroyer and taken to the sanctuary of Gibraltar.

"Oh, we had some party that night. It was a riot. Our Captain jumped up on a table and led the chorus of 'Shenandoah'."

"The Chief Engineer shouted in my ear, 'It's a good job he was back on the drink the night we were torpedoed,'"

That was our Mate's story in praise of drink.

50

DRUNKEN SAILOR IN MID-AIR

"Anyone who's drunk won't be allowed on the plane."

While at sea mariners have to put up with one another. They do it for the sake of getting the ship or yacht safely home. However, end-of-voyage drinking sessions, whether on board the vessel or in some dockside bar, can spawn old resentments and even fights.

The possibility of such rows became a problem for the Ellerman shipping line on those ships that traded between Canada and India. The crews were Lascars, sailors from the Indian sub-continent. The officers were mostly British. They did six months duty and were then replaced by a new contingent. Gibraltar was the staging post. A small aircraft was chartered to ferry men and baggage between there and the UK.

The trouble was that some fellows being relieved began to celebrate as soon as they got off the ship. Even before the plane took off they were under the weather.

On one occasion, while the plane was over the mountain peaks of the Pyrennees, one of the Fifth Engineers staggered up the aisle. He bore a grudge against the Second

Engineer so he clocked him. A fist fight broke out involving four or five men.

The pilot looked over his shoulder at the melee and became concerned for the safety of the aircraft. He took the precaution of landing in Bordeaux. The plane didn't take off until the following morning when the combatants had sobered up.

The Ellerman line was far from pleased at the additional cost this episode entailed. Ships' captain on the route were warned that anyone who was visibly drunk should on no account be allowed to board the plane home from Gibraltar.

The Captain of our ship didn't welcome this responsibility. He was a small, nervous sort of man whose hobby was knitting and who dyed his toenails. He had a fear of flying. We had done our six months on the run and now, approaching Gibraltar, were looking forward to being relieved and flying back home.

Almost as soon as we docked in the shadow of the Rock our replacements came on board. We handed over to them and then made our way down the gangway lugging our baggage.

There at the bottom of the gangway stood our Captain. His small face was strained. He kept calling out: "Anyone who gets drunk won't be allowed on the plane. Anyone who gets drunk won't be allowed on the plane."

However there was a delay at the airport before our baggage could be loaded on to the plane. This allowed some fellows to buy small flat bottles of Spanish brandy and stow them discreetly in their jackets.

Our anxious Captain stood by the set of steps into the plane, looking intently at men walking across the tarmac. He himself was last on board and sat up beside the pilot.

We took off and gained height over Spain. Soon the bottles of brandy were being passed around behind the Captain's back. Fortunately, there was no suppressed rancour among our group of officers and no reason to expect any blows being exchanged.

Eventually, our small plane cleared the Pyrennees and droned on over France. By that time five or six of our fellows were pleasantly merry.

Then, with about half an hour to go before landing at Stansted Airport, there began a chorus of that old sea shanty, "What will be do with the drunken sailor". It got louder and more boisterous.

The pilot turned around and grinned. But our Captain held up a hand, as if to warn that such singing might endanger the plane. The singers took no notice of him. Now mouths opened wide and brandy-hoarsened voices bellowed out the refrain: "Way hay and up she rises, way hay and up she rises, early in the morning."

The signing stopped only when the plane began its descent and we were asked to fasten our seat belts.

When the plane landed our Captain rushed out the door, relieved that the ordeal was over. The rest eased themselves out the door, in good humour. I was the last to leave and the pilot, a cheery English fellow, turned to me and said: "Your captain was acting strangely. Had too much to drink, had he?"

51

ALL-IRELAND FEVER
IN THE TROPICS

"This is the wrong time for some fool to send out an SOS"

The two Radio Officers, faces red with perspiration and anxiety, sat in the sweltering radio room of the passenger ship. The Chief Radio Officer used his tapered, nail-bitten fingers to delicately rotate the tuning control on one of the big marine receivers. Even though it was nine o'clock at night the equatorial heat was claustrophobic. There is no air-conditioning on the *Amra*, sailing off the coast of Somaliland, bound for Mombasa, Zanzibar and Dar es Salaam from Bombay.

The Chief was in a bad temper. He had been severely reprimanded by the Captain for unseemly behaviour with a lady passenger in the First Class bar; she had objected to his alcohol-driven impulse to thrust his hand under her skirt. In a vicious rage he had flung things violently about his cabin and, in doing so, lost his full set of dentures. Now the mouth on his gin-soaked face was a sunken hole.

"Radio Brazzaville must be there somewhere. I tuned it in last night," I said impatiently. I was the pimply-faced junior, on my first ship and first voyage.

"Don't try to hassle me. I was at sea long before you ever heard of a Morse key."

"The All-Ireland will be over by the time..."

"Shut your trap, for Christ's sake."

As the tuning marker glided slowly along the long yellow dial an incongruous procession of sounds filled the air: balalaika music from Moscow; the sonorous, measured tones from the Voice of America; the melodic sound of Georges Guétary singing on Radio France International; followed by a speaking voice that sounded like elastic being rapidly twanged that may have been Hindi or Urdu.

"Hold on, hold on!" yelled the Chief. He turned up the volume control and, like the genie out of the bottle, the voice of Micheál O'Hehir flooded into that radio room. Curses and blasphemies of relief and excitement. The Chief had been so long East of Suez that he has lost much contact with Ireland and has only a tenuous knowledge of the hurling scene. But he was as elated as I was; I had seen both teams in action several times just before being posted to Eastern service with the Marconi Company.

This was 1956. It's many years and many miles away from the era of satellite TV and the Internet which today make seeing and hearing the All-Ireland a commonplace experience even in the most remote corners of the globe.

In those bad old days Rádio Éireann, which never broadcast on world-spanning short wave, had an arrangement with the colonial administration in the French Congo to rebroadcast the All-Ireland from Brazzaville's powerful transmitter. This was sent out on to the airwaves on the

Mondays after the big game. In distant and sometimes lonely corners of the earth, Irish people sat around radio sets, patiently trying to tune in the oft-wavering signals from equatorial Africa.

I told the Chief about the two great sides that squared up to one another for that titanic hurling final of 1956. Stalwarts like the Rackard brothers and Ned Wheeler were among the many accomplished and powerful hurlers on the Wexford side. Cork had the stellar Christy Ring in action, along with outstanding players like Willie John Daly and Josie Hartnett.

When the Artane Boys Band finished the national anthem, the roar of over 80,000 spectators came pouring out of the receiver in a huge landslide of sound. As the match got under way the rapid-fire commentary transported us back to a scene remote from the teeming streets of our home port of Bombay. The mind's eye pictured vividly the see-saw of the game, the shoulder to shoulder races for the ball, the rapid swing of hurleys, the ball soaring through the air with the packed stands as background.

The thunderous applause that greeted the goals scored by Wexford and by Cork made the loudspeaker vibrate. The names of the players rang out in the tropic night: Nick O'Donnell, Jimmy Brohan, Tim Flood, Matt Fouhy. The occasional Lascar seaman, padding barefooted past the door on the way to or from the bridge-deck above, glanced in with curious, dark-brown eyes.

Wexford were well on top in the early part of the second half. Then Christy Ring scored a goal from a 21-yard free. Just at that moment several large locust-like creatures flew into the radio room, whizzing round the lights, flitting from bulkhead to bulkhead. We were near the coast and these repulsive creatures often flew far out to sea.

"Get out, you fuckers," shouted the Chief. He grabbed the radio log-book and used it as a swatter. I put the telegram receipt book to the same use. We flailed furiously about at these elusive African interlopers, accompanied by the urgent high-pitched voice of Mícheál O'Hehir. It was as if we too were playing at Croke Park. Eventually we scored several hits apiece, squashing these large insects, and driving the survivors out the door into the night.

In the final quarter Wexford were ahead but Paddy Barry brought the sides level with a goal and then Christy Ring put Cork ahead with a point. The perspiration poured off us as we listened with absolute intensity to every puck of this great game. Wexford powered back and were ahead with only a few minutes to go.

We nearly missed the legendary save by the Wexford goalkeeper Art Foley when Ring, for once breaking free from Bobby Rackard, fired a shot at goal. Just before that pivotal moment Radio Brazzaville faded. It may have been the heat in the receiver that caused the signal to go out of tune. Another station that sounded very like All India Radio came into being; Mícheál O'Hehir's voice was replaced by that of Lata Mangeshkar, then and for many decades one of India's most popular female vocalists.

"Get to fuck out of that," shouted the Chief in a vindictive Belfast tone. Then, biting his lips with concentration, with the sensitive skill born of years of experience, he turned the tuning control slowly and coaxed Radio Brazzaville and the All Ireland final back into the receiver and the radio room of the *Amra*. After Foley's save Wexford surged forward and the redoubtable Nick Rackard wrapped it up with a thundering goal and Tom Dixon added a point just before the final whistle blew.

We were both limp, drained of energy.

"I'll die if I don't get a drink right away," said the Chief. Even though we were supposed to be keeping radio watch on 500 kc/s, the international distress frequency, we abandoned the radio room and repaired to the Chief's chaotic cabin.

"No bugger has the right to send out an SOS when the All-Ireland is on," said the Chief with a toothless grin as he poured himself a large gin.

52

WARTIME CATASTROPHE IN THE INDIAN OCEAN

A horrifying mistake in the midst of calamity

The sinking of the *Tilawa* in November 1942 by a Japanese submarine was a traumatic event in the history of the World War Two in the Indian Ocean. She was a deck-passenger ship carrying hundreds of Indian passengers crowded together in bunks and hammocks in the lower decks.

The ship was some 600 kilometres east of the island of Socotra when she was torpedoed. Of the 732 passengers, about 250 lost their lives, while 28 of the 222 crew perished. Most of the survivors were picked up by a British cruiser, the *HMS Birmingham*.

Several years later, in the bar of our own ship, I came across a British engineer who claimed he had been a passenger on that ill-fated vessel. He had drink taken when he told me such a harrowing story and I had some doubts about it.

He said that when he heard the first explosion he put on his life-jacket and ran out on deck.

"Oh it was was absolute panic. The lifeboats were being rushed, people trampled on in the stampede. I met one of the deck officers and asked him if I could help. He told me to stand by one of the lifeboats, to try to keep order while people were put on board.

I got into a terrible rage when I saw women and children being pushed aside by fellows only out to save their own skins. I had a Belgian pistol and I threatened some fellows with it."

In an open passageway nearby he saw some suitcases lying on the deck. They looked expensive, as if they belonged to the few First Class passengers. At that moment a small Indian man dressed in white cotton ran forward and started to open one.

"I was sure he was looting. I roared at him to get back or I'd shoot him. He waved his hands. shouting something in an Indian language. I only intended to fire a warning shot but he suddenly jumped to one side and the bullet caught him in the middle of his forehead. He staggered away and then fell backwards over the side, into the sea below."

Just then a young girl of about twelve came running along. '"Have you seen my father?" she asked in English. When she saw the suitcase she went straight over, opened it quickly and took out a small roll wrapped in cloth.

"We need our money. If you see my father tell him I have it." And she scurried away.

He told me that he was utterly distraught. He just stood there stunned. There was further uproar when a second torpedo struck and the ship then began to go down.

He stayed on board almost to the end, threw his pistol into the sea and then climbed on to a life raft with two or three others.

Lifeboats and rafts bobbed around in the sea along with bodies and debris. He wondered if the body of a man with a bullet hole in his head would be found, but it was not. On the morning of the 25th the British warship appeared and rescued most of the survivors to take them back to Bombay.

"I went around the decks, keeping an eye out for that young girl but I couldn't find her. I felt so bad. I don't know if she had survived but I had killed her father by mistake."

I was both shocked and intrigued by this tragic story. I asked an Indian friend who worked for the shipping agents in Bombay, Mackinnon and Mackenzie, to search for the man's name on the *Tilawa's* passenger list. He couldn't find it. But he said that war-time chaos had swamped the booking and embarcation process, with last-minute additions and cancellations. One couldn't be sure. So some mystery and uncertainty surrounds this heart-rending tale.

53

HE HAD A JOLLY GOD WAR

Ended up bloated from guzzling and gorging

World War Two in the British merchant marine is now no more than a very distant memory in the minds of those who are still alive today. However, when I went to sea in the 1950s I came across many who had lived through it. For them the war at sea was a time of fear and, in some cases, suffering.

Some carried physical and emotional scars. One ship's Mate still kept his arms about his lifejacket as he went to sleep. On two occasions it had helped save him after his cargo ship had been torpedoed and he found himself bobbing around in the sea.

A Chief Engineer I knew, a genial Scotsman, always stood at the door of anyone's cabin rather than coming in and sitting down. In a terrifying wartime experience he had been trapped in his own cabin as flames engulfed the ship; he only managed to escape by squeezing through the small porthole.

These survivors used to say things like, "Oh, I had a bad war" or "Oh, I hadn't an easy war." Yet I came across a most

168

extraordinary story of a man who had what the British might call "a jolly good war".

Our Purser, a stout, amiable Englishman, had been on a refrigerated merchant vessel that was commandeered by the British Navy at the beginning of the war. Loaded with food and fresh produce, drink and tobacco, it was sent to Gibraltar as a supply ship. Its role was to replenish the stores of warships from the North Atlantic and the Mediterranean. These vessels came in to the sanctuary of Gibraltar. Many were sea-battered after weeks ploughing the waves. Some were battle-scarred.

"We were permanently stationed there for the duration," he told me. "When our stores ran low we ourselves were re-supplied by ships sent out from the UK."

Inevitably, there was a certain amount of fairly small-scale pilfering among the ship's company.

"It was hard to resist temptation," he said, explaining that his principal duty was keeping records of all the range of supplies. He spent a good deal of time alone down in the holds with notebook and pencil and provision sheets. A hearty eater and drinker at the best of times, he now found himself in an Aladdin's cave of meats, fish, fruit and vegetables, tobacco and a range of beers and spirits.

"I put on a lot of weight and I drank a fair bit too," he said. "I wasn't falling down drunk, but I was pleasantly tipsy most of the time."

He was a smoker and he regularly helped himself to those sealed tins of 50 Players Navy Cut.

He loved the sunny climate. During off-duty times he soaked up the sun until he was brown as a nut. Sitting outside cafes he often watched the pale, gaunt faces of men off the warships; they had spent days on end being tossed around the wild waves of the North Atlantic while chasing U-Boats or being machine-gunned from the air.

He found plenty of opportunities to become intimate with women. His love affairs were certainly helped by the fact that he was able to bring presents of bottles of whisky or cartons of cigarettes. "I was never without a girl friend during the years spent in Gibraltar," he told me.

However, the war slowly drew to a close. Our jolly Purser, fat from eating and drinking, had to face the unwelcome reality of returning home from sunny Gibraltar to grey, dreary Britain.

"OK, like everybody else I was glad the war was over. But in all honesty I have to say that my role in World War Two was four years of food, drink, tobacco, sex and sunshine. I would have to admit that I had a fabulous war."

54

MUSLIM PILGRIMS REVERED JESUS CHRIST

"You chaps need to be careful."

At a time of tension between the Muslim and Christian traditions it's helpful to remember that Muslims regard Jesus Christ as an important prophet.

This fact was unknown to the European officers of the *Sirdhana,* a deck-passenger ship of the British India shipping company when it set sail from the port of Karachi. We were bound for Jeddah, in Saudi Arabia.

At that port on the Red Sea the ship was to take on board Muslim pilgrims who had completed the pilgrimage to the holy city of Mecca. We were to take them back to Chittagong, at the top of the Bay of Bengal.

On the voyage to Jeddah the ship was empty. On the fore part of the promenade deck the European officers played table tennis. The slight rolling of the ship as we ploughed along the Arabian Sea called for some special skills. Both winners and losers, all Christians and mostly British, gave vent to loud oaths and blasphemies during games.

As a result, as we neared Jeddah, our Captain called us all to his cabin for a meeting.

"You chaps will need to be careful with your language when our Muslim pilgrims come on board," he said in a fatherly tone. "They don't like to hear the name of Jesus Christ bandied about, as he is of some significance to them."

We noted his comments and decided to be careful about our language when the pilgrims boarded.

They lived in one of the most impoverished countries in the world, Bangladesh. Many had saved and scrimped for years to put together the cost of the pilgrimage. For them, a visit to the holy sites around Mecca was to be the culmination of a lifetime of religious devotion.

When our ship docked at the crowded port of Jeddah we looked down on a most disturbing sight. The pilgrims, some skeletal and many in poor shape, were being harshly corralled on the dockside by the Saudi police, in the searing heat.

As a mark of the completion of the pilgrimage the men had dyed their beards with henna, a reddish-brown colour.

When our gangways went down, they staggered on board. Some were so weak that they had to be helped. Our doctors and nurses began their treatments even before the full complement of passengers had boarded our big, white-painted passenger ship.

The pilgrims were led by an imam, who had a large impressive beard and a powerful voice. Early each morning he went into the Purser's office and called the faithful to prayer over the big loudspeakers of the public address system. My religious tolerance was put to the test, since after six hours duty on the night watch as Second Radio Officer, I was just about to fall asleep in my bunk when the loud calls to prayer boomed.

The promenade deck was a principal area of devotion. Prayer mats were laid on the wooden deck in orderly lines and the pilgrims knelt and bent forward in unison, while the imam intoned the prayers.

Illness, much of it made worse by malnutrition, ravaged the passengers. It was considered fortunate that there were only four deaths. The bodies, wrapped in canvas and weighted with lead, were put into a chute on the poop deck aft. The imam intoned prayers and the bodies slid into the Indian Ocean.

When at last we reached Chittagong the weary pilgrims made their way down the gangways onto the dockside.

The next day the covers were taken off the table tennis table and we resumed our noisy tournaments. Our use of blasphemous language also resumed.

55

A SPIRITED CHRISTMAS

Plum pudding a fire hazard

Christmas Day at sea! Every sailor seems to have a yarn to spin about it.

My story of Christmas at sea took place on board a small, down-at-heel cargo vessel. We were in the North Atlantic, heading for New York. Since we left Liverpool the decks had been rising and falling, sloping and slanting as we tossed through one storm after another.

However, many on board were consoling themselves by copious drinking. This was because part of our cargo was a consignment of Scotch whisky for the United States. This proved to be an irresistible temptation to our motley, rag-tag crew. Cases of it were expertly stolen early in the voyage. As far as the consumption of alcohol went, every day was Christmas Day.

When the day itself arrived there was no expectation that we were going to get a sumptuous Christmas meal. The food on board that dingy ship was anything but appetising.

The provision of food wasn't helped by the fact that the two cooks disliked one another. One was a small fellow from Bootle who scurried about the galley like a bad-tempered rat. The other "chef" was an elderly Londoner with a shock of grey hair.

This Christmas Day their animosity in the galley was made worse by the fact that they were both sullenly drunk.

In the saloon the Captain, Chief Engineer, Mate and myself sat waiting for our Christmas dinner. We could hear the abusive shouting coming from the galley, pots being thumped about.

"Peace on earth to men of good will," said the Chief Engineer solemnly. He was an elderly man who was given to sarcasm.

The Captain was a fat, jolly fellow but he was hungry and his temper became frayed as we waited and waited.

"I'll go in there and give both of them a boot up the backside apiece if we don't get something to eat soon," he snapped at our gay steward. This individual had marked the festival by donning a bright green jacket and a pair of plum-coloured trousers.

Eventually our steward began to ferry in plates of turkey and ham. These delicacies were hidden under a hideous thick gravy that had the appearance of a cowpat. When this was taken off the turkey portions were found to have been barely cooked. The ham, on the other hand, had been par-boiled to the point of squashy disintegration.

The Captain, who had an indiscriminate appetite, wolfed the mess down. The rest of us just picked at it.

"At least we might have a bit of plum pudding," said the Mate hopefully, as the steward took the plates away.

Then we heard a yell of alarm from the galley. The next thing the steward came rushing in, head and shoulders arched back, arms extended full length, bearing a ball of blue flame on a platter. We pushed back our chairs and stood up. The black object at the centre of the flame was our Christmas pudding. It had obviously been drowned in stolen whisky. The steward flapped at it with a dirty dish-cloth but this only caused the flames to leap up alarmingly high.

Then the Captain took charge. He seized a big jug of water and poured it over the flame. The sodden, smoking pudding looked like a cannon ball come to rest after an explosive trajectory. A cloud of blue alcohol vapour rose up. It entered the lungs of the Chief Engineer, who suffered badly from emphysema. He got into a sickening bout of heaving, gurgling, wheezing and coughing.

When it died down the Captain looked at the pudding and ordered: "Take the bugger away."

The next thing we heard the heavy thunk of our Christmas pudding being thrown into the big metal waste bin in the galley.

That was our Christmas meal. As we filed out of the saloon, the Chief Engineer intoned, "We thank Thee Lord for Thy bounteous gifts of which we have partaken this blessed day."

56

FEAR AND UNEASE OFF CAPE HATTERAS

Passing a graveyard in the dead of night

The Captain's mood changed on this dark and windy night as our ship neared Cape Hatteras. Normally he was jolly and relaxed, a confident seafarer who allowed nothing to bother him. Now he started to become tense and tetchy. He kept moving from the chartroom to the wing of the bridge and back again, his binoculars slung round his neck.

He leaned over the chart, adjusting the angled light so that its bright beam shone directly down on that dominant feature of the North Carolina coastline, Cape Hatteras.

It stuck out dangerously into Atlantic Ocean. But the real hazards were the shallow sandbars beneath the surging currents in its vicinity. Our course should take us well clear of them but the Captain was uneasy.

"Any sign of the light yet, Third Mate?" he called out, as if the Third Mate had some responsibility for actually making it appear out of the gloom. The lighthouse on Hatteras Island is one of the tallest in the world with a powerful beam seen from miles away. It had been erected because so many ships had come to grief in this area that it became known as the "Graveyard of the Atlantic".

"Anything on the radar yet, Sparks?" he asked me, as I peered into the screen. The radar was on the 40 mile range but I could see nothing. I had become slightly infected by his anxiety, afraid the radar might develop a fault at the very time it was most needed.

It was midnight and the Second Mate came on watch. The Captain conferred with him and together they looked at the course laid off on the chart. The Second Mate, usually a placid fellow, began to suck his teeth as he studied the chart. We were in a place of strong colliding currents, where the warm Gulf Stream meets the icy Labrador Current. He and the Captain went out on the wing.

The Third Mate came over to the radar.

"If we don't see Cape Hatteras soon our Captain will have a baby," he said with an attempt at humour.

Then, to my relief, the sweep of the rotating cursor on the radar began to pick up the orange echoes of the jutting point of land on the North Carolina coastline. I called the Captain. "Good. Good. Good man, Sparks," he said, tapping me in the shoulder as if to congratulate me. He went back out on to the wing. Some time later his voice could be heard shouting from the windy darkness. "I can see the bugger now."

I joined the three of them outside. Even in the dark I could tell that the Captain's stressful mood had been lifted by the tiny, regular flashes of light away at the very edge of the pitch darkness.

For the next hour or more, on radar and by sight, we watched Cape Hatteras slowly come abeam of us and then begin to recede. The Captain spent a lot of time on the wing, watching the pin points of light getting fainter until they had almost disappeared.

When he eventually returned to the chartroom he was his own jolly self. Since he was not a man to hide the disasters of his life at sea, I wondered if he might launch into a highly coloured story of some unfortunate incident about Cape Hatteras.

But, if he had some tale of marine calamity to tell, he kept it to himself. Instead he grinned impishly. "Next port New Orleans. We might get a bit of black ham there, eh?" he said, using his term for sex with dark-skinned women, to which he seemed partial.

57

TRAGEDY AVERTED WHEN SHIP WENT ABLAZE

Nordic nerves saved lives in Skaubryn drama

SOS, SOS. As soon as I switched on the receiver to begin the six-hour radio watch I became aware of a desperate drama taking place on the far side of the Arabian Sea. The date was 11 March 1958. The Norwegian-registered emigrant ship, the *Skaubryn*, was sending out distress signals. A fire was engulfing the ship.

I sat there glued to the international distress frequency, listening to the calls for help in Morse Code. The news from the stricken vessel was that the order had been given to abandon ship and the lifeboats were being swung out.

The distress calls were being answered by a British ship, the *City of Sydney*, which apparently was not far from the blazing vessel, off the coast of Somalia.

As soon as I got the chance I ran up to the bridge of our vessel, the deck-passenger ship *Aronda,* to tell the Second Mate. We were too far away to be of any assistance as we were hundreds of miles away, off the Gujarat coast of India heading for Karachi from Colombo.

We knew the *Skaubyrn*. Several times we had been anchored alongside her in Colombo harbour. She was an elegant, white passenger vessel of around 9,700 tons that carried emigrants from Europe to Australia.

From the faint Morse signals I gathered that the *Skaubryn* had been abandoned and those in the lifeboats had been picked up by the British ship. An Italian liner, the *Roma,* was drawing near.

Only later did we learn that the ship was carrying 2,188 emigrants from Germany and Malta, men, women and children. A disconnected fuel line spuirted a gushing cascade of oil on to red-hot exhaust pipes in the engine room. In minutes the ship was engulfed by an uncontrollable furnace.

Women were sobbing and children crying as the lifeboats were quickly prepared. Some were boarded by a small number of men who panicked. However, the stolid Norwegian crewmen hauled them out and took control with dour efficiency.

Of the 1,288 passengers and 200 crew not a single life was lost in the raging inferno. Nobody was even injured. The only casualty was a German man who suffered a heart attack and died.

Only 35 minutes elapsed from the start of the fire until the Captain, Alf Haakon Faeste, the last to leave, slid down a rope while clutching the ship's log book.

The distraught passengers, many of whom had lost all their belongings, were full of praise for the kindness shown to them on the British ship, and later the Italian liner to which they were transferred.

An attempt was made to tow the smouldering wreck of the *Skaubryn* to Aden but she was too badly damaged. She broke in two and sank.

There was widespread praise for the way the Norwegian crew had comported themselves in getting all passengers to safety in the most appalling circumstances. They had shown great courage and discipline in the midst of calamity.

Our true-Brit Captain pronounced: "Norwegians are rather dull fellows but, by gosh, when it comes to an emergency at sea they are no better chaps to have around. They do what they have to do without creating any kind of fuss."

58

CAPTAIN WHO SHOWED WOMEN THE STARS

Lady friends on the bridge after midnight

We learned that the Captain of the Italian cruise liner, *Costa Concordia* had his girl friend with him on the bridge when the vessel crunched on to rocks off the Italian coast.

It's not a good idea for any Captain to have a lady friend on the bridge when the ship is negotiating a narrow passage or manouevring to come alongside.

There's a time and a place for that kind of thing. I knew of an amorous Captain who sailed about the Indian Ocean and was noted for taking carefully selected women passengers up to the bridge deck. But he did it only when the ship was well away from land. And, for reasons of propriety and romance, only in the small hours of the night.

The Second Officer of our ship had sailed with this particular Captain for two years so he was able to spin some colourful yarns about him.

"We called him Captain Starlight," he said. "He was good-looking fellow in his mid-fifties. He certainly had a roving eye."

That ship had accommodation for only fifty First Class passengers, mostly Europeans and wealthy Indians. There were always five or six women among them, some very attractive types in early middle age, fairly well seasoned in the love parade. They would be travelling unaccompanied to Mombasa or Colombo or Bombay or Dar es Salaam.

Apparently Captain Starlight had a well-developed ability to sense which women were most likely to be open to a brief shipboard romance. He would see to it that they were put sitting at his table in the saloon.

On the first or second evening at sea he would go down to the First Class bar for a social drink, dressed in his smart tropical uniform. He would soon get talking to the woman he had his eye on. This amiable man had a way with him. He would ask the woman about herself and listen with interest to what she had to say.

The conversation would inevitably turn to his role as Captain. This is when he went into a familiar routine, waxing lyrical about how exciting it was to stand on the wing of the bridge sometime after midnight, looking up at the stars. They were so bright in the tropic night that they seemed to lower themselves towards earth. He was eloquent, even poetic.

More often then not the woman might say something like, "That sounds marvellous. Maybe I could join you."

He would say, "Of course. But let's keep it between ourselves." This gave their post-midnight tryst an air of secrecy and adventure. She would be waiting for him alone on the promenade deck about 1.00 a.m. He'd come down and lead the way up to the bridge deck.

That's the way it was, according to the Second Officer. The two would go out onto the wing of the bridge and stay there for a while, gazing up at the heavens until the Captain suggested a warming drink. He had a spacious, comfortable cabin behind the bridge, with a living area and a bedroom. It would be five or six in the morning before he led her down to the promenade deck and she went off to her cabin. This pattern might last a day or two or more until they reached port and the woman disembarked.

The Second Officer said: "Oh, indeed, during the time I sailed with him he showed several women the stars – I remember two good-looking English memsahibs and a glamorous Hungarian woman with flaming red hair. And a stunning Indian actress, famous not only for her beauty but for her promiscuity."

Then he chuckled and said, "That man should be awarded the gold medal of the Royal Astronomical Society for promoting interest in the stars."

59

THE LURE OF FAR-AWAY PLACES

The enticing call fading into the night

My brother Tom and I both went to sea. Young fellows like ourselves longed to get away from the bleak, impoverished Ireland of the 1950s.

Our notion of the world outside Ireland was largely provided by Hollywood films, newsreels and adventure stories borrowed from the town library. There, the triangular white sails of Arab dhows moved across the Indian Ocean or Chinese sampans rested in the harbour in Hong Kong.

Those remote places seemed to have a lot of white sandy beaches fringed by palm trees. Sweating men in straw hats carried huge hanks of bananas on their shoulders, while women in sarongs and saris radiated an exotic attraction. Going to sea seemed like the best way to experience these exotic worlds.

Our yearning was heightened in a strange way by the fact that our house, near the sugar factory outside the town of Thurles in County Tipperary, was within sight and sound of the main railway line between Dublin and Cork. The tracks were about a mile away, on an embankment.

From the window of our upstairs bedroom we could get a brief glimpse of trains as they rumbled past up and down the line. We used to imagine that they were carrying people on their way to colourful bazaars where men wore turbans and women covered their faces up to their eyes.

We loved to watch them going pass. The one that most intrigued us was the Dublin-Cork mail train that passed by at around midnight, going south.

Since the Leaving Certificate exam was upon us we were often up at midnight trying to study. Sometimes we would go to the window and open it gently. First we could hear the diesel engine heaving and throbbing. Then came the rattle of steel wheels clacking over the rail-joinings.

In those days there was little or no public lighting and the midnight countryside seemed to be always in pitch blackness. It made it easier to see the row of orange windows moving along like some sort of glow-worm. It soon disappeared from view into the darkness.

What didn't go away for a long time was the sound, especially if it was a still night. It kept on and on. It seemed as if a hallow boom enveloped the dark countryside all round. After a while it declined to a gentle rumbling. It got fainter, but very slowly. We listened intently until it faded to nothingness.

It stirred in us a longing to go away, to see the world. It seemed like a beginning of long journeys to distant places, whether by train or bus, by plane or ship. We were intrigued about far-away places with strange-sounding names. We had read the poem in Irish that begins "*Thánig long as Valparaiso*" – "a ship arrived from Valparaiso" – and wondered if we would ever see that place.

The sound of the midnight mail train seemed like a siren call, an invitation to go seek out strange seas and lands.

My brother and I achieved our aim to see such places. Like quite a few others in Ireland we did it by joining the Marconi Company as seafaring Radio Officers. We travelled far and wide over the seven seas and many of the lands and cities bound by them.

Now, many years later, I've forgotten much of the sound and bustle and smell of cities like Bombay – now called Mumbai – or Karachi, the reek of mangrove swamps in Nigeria, or the sight of icebergs off the coast of Canada. But in my inner ear I can still hear the sound of that night mail train going away into the night.